FEDERAL PROGRAMS AND POLICIES FOR HIGHWAYS

SELECT ASPECTS AND ROLES

TRANSPORTATION INFRASTRUCTURE - ROADS, HIGHWAYS, BRIDGES, AIRPORTS AND MASS TRANSIT

Additional books in this series can be found on Nova's website under the Series tab.

Additional e-books in this series can be found on Nova's website under the e-books tab.

TRANSPORTATION ISSUES, POLICIES AND R&D

Additional books in this series can be found on Nova's website under the Series tab.

Additional e-books in this series can be found on Nova's website under the e-books tab.

TRANSPORTATION INFRASTRUCTURE - ROADS, HIGHWAYS, BRIDGES, AIRPORTS AND MASS TRANSIT

FEDERAL PROGRAMS AND POLICIES FOR HIGHWAYS

SELECT ASPECTS AND ROLES

EVAN D. CAMPBELL

AND

EDWARD SANCHEZ

EDITORS

nova
publishers

New York

LIBRARY OF CONGRESS CATALOGING-IN-PUBLICATION DATA

ISBN: 978-1-62257-755-2

Published by Nova Science Publishers, Inc. † New York

CONTENTS

PREFACE

This book examines select aspects and the role of federal programs and policies for highway infrastructure. Issues discussed include the federal excise tax on gasoline and the Highway Trust Fund; the role of the Environmental Review Process in federally funded highway projects; the emergency relief program and federal-aid highway assistance for disaster-damaged roads and bridges; tolling of interstate highways; broadband telecommunications as vital for improving state and local systems for traffic management and public safety; revised federal standards for traffic signs; and a legislative history of federal aid to roads and highways since the 18th century.

Chapter 1 - Excise taxes have long been a part of our country's revenue history. In the field of gasoline taxation, the states led the way with Oregon enacting the first tax on motor fuels in 1919. By 1932, all states and the District of Columbia had followed suit with tax rates that ranged between two and seven cents per gallon.

The federal government first imposed its excise tax on gasoline at a one-cent per gallon rate in 1932. The gas tax was enacted to correct a federal budgetary imbalance. It continued to support general revenue during World War II and the Korean War.

Economists know the gasoline excise tax as a "manufacturer's excise tax" because the government imposes it at production (i.e., the producer, refiner, or importer) for efficiency in collection. Particularly in the short run, when the demand for gasoline is relatively inelastic, economists recognize that any increase in the gasoline tax ultimately falls on the consumer.

The Highway Revenue Act of 1956 established the federal Highway Trust Fund (HTF) for the direct purpose of funding the construction of an interstate highway system, and aiding in the finance of primary, secondary, and urban routes. Each time Congress has extended the Highway Trust Fund it has also extended the federal excise tax on gasoline.

For FY2011, the Congressional Budget Office estimated that revenues and interest credited to the Highway Trust Fund will total $36.9 billion, which will be divided into the Highway Account ($31.8 billion) and the Mass Transit Account ($5.1 billion).

CBO also estimated that the fund's three primary revenue sources and their yields will be the gasoline tax ($24.0 billion), the diesel tax ($8.7 billion), and the tax on trucks and trailers ($2.2 billion). On September 16, 2011, President Obama signed H.R. 2887, Surface and Air Transportation Programs Extension Act of 2011 (P.L. 112-30), which extended, through March 31, 2012, current surface transportation programs and the motor fuel, heavy truck, and truck tire taxes that support the HTF.

On November 9, 2011, the Senate Environment and Public Works Committee marked up and reported favorable on the highway provisions of S. 1813, the Moving Ahead for Progress in the 21st Century Act (MAP-21). S. 1813 is a two-year reauthorization bill for FY2012-FY2013 that basically funds the Federal-Aid Highway Program at the baseline level, adjusted for inflation.

This bill would also make substantial changes to the structure, formulas, and funding distribution of the federal highway program. As of February 7, 2012, all committees of jurisdiction had marked up their titles. On March 1, 2012, these titles were folded into S.Amdt. 1761 to S. 1813.

On March 5, 2012, in response to a request from Senate Majority Leader Harry Reid, the Congressional Budget Office (CBO) issued estimates for S. 1813, MAP-21, with amendment. CBO estimated that implementing the bill would have discretionary costs of $47.0 billion over the FY2012-FY2017 period.

In addition, CBO estimated that implementing the provisions of the bill for the remainder of FY2012 and for FY2013 would result in an end-of-year balance in 2013 of approximately $2 billion in the highway account of the HTF and about $3 billion in the transit account of the HTF.

On April 1, 2012, current surface transportation programs are scheduled to expire, and taxes that support the Highway Trust Fund are scheduled to expire or decline. The primary revenue source for the HTF, the gasoline tax, will decline from 18.4 cents per gallon to 4.3 cents per gallon.

Chapter 2 - This testimony reviews the status of the Highway Trust Fund and examines three questions facing the Congress:

- How much should the federal government spend on highways?
- How should the federal government direct the use of those funds?
- How should the federal government raise those funds?

Chapter 3 - Under programs administered by the Department of Transportation's (DOT's) Federal Highway Administration (FHWA), certain highway and bridge projects may be eligible for federal funding. Project approval and the receipt of federal funds are conditioned on the project sponsor (e.g., a local public works or state transportation agency) meeting certain standards and complying with federal law. Activities necessary to demonstrate compliance with those requirements may be completed at various stages of project development. Although the names of each stage may vary from state to state, project development generally includes the following: planning, preliminary design and environmental review, final design and rights-of-way acquisition, construction, and facility operation and maintenance.

When there is debate over the time it takes to complete federal highway projects, the environmental review stage has been a primary focus of congressional attention concerning legislative options to speed project delivery. The current process includes activities necessary to demonstrate that all potential project-related impacts to the human, natural, and cultural environment are identified; effects of those impacts are taken into consideration (among other factors such as economic or community benefits) before a final decision is made; the public is included in that decision-making process; and all state, tribal, or federal compliance requirements applicable as a result of the project's environmental impacts are, or will be, met.

Compliance requirements depend on site-specific factors, including the size and scope of the project, and whether and to what degree it may affect resources such as parks, historic sites, water resources, wetlands, or urban communities. For all proposed federal-aid highway projects, however, some level of review will be required under the National Environmental Policy Act of 1969 (NEPA, 42 U.S.C. §4321 et seq.). Broadly, NEPA requires federal agencies to consider the environmental effects of an action before proceeding with it and to involve the public in the decision-making process.

The time it takes to complete the NEPA process is often the focus of debate over project delays attributable to the overall environmental review stage. However, the majority of FHWA-approved projects require limited documentation or analyses under NEPA. Further, when environmental requirements have caused project delays, requirements established under laws other than NEPA have generally been the source. This calls into question the degree to which the NEPA compliance process is a significant source of delay in completing either the environmental review process or overall project delivery. Causes of delay that have been identified are more often tied to local/state and project-specific factors, primarily local/state agency priorities, project funding levels, local opposition to a project, project complexity, or late changes in project scope. Further, approaches that have been found to expedite environmental reviews involve procedures that local and state transportation agencies may implement currently, such as efficient coordination of inter-agency involvement; early and continued involvement with stakeholders interested in the project; and identifying environmental issues and require-ments early in project development.

Bills in the House and Senate (the American Energy and Infrastructure Jobs Act of 2012 (H.R. 7) and Moving Ahead for Progress in the 21st Century (MAP-21; S. 1813)) would reauthorize DOT programs. Both include provisions intended to expedite project delivery by changing elements of the environmental review process, particularly NEPA requirements. This report provides information on existing NEPA and environmental review requirements, particularly requirements that may be subject to change under the House and Senate proposals.

Chapter 4 - The major highways and bridges damaged during Hurricane Irene in 2011and the I-35W bridge collapse in Minneapolis of August 1, 2007 are part of the federal-aid highway system and were therefore eligible for assistance under the Federal Highway Administration's (FHWA's) Emergency Relief Program (ER). Following a natural disaster or catastrophic failure (such as the I-35W bridge), ER funds are made available for both emergency repairs and restoration of federal-aid highway facilities to pre-disaster conditions.

The ER program is administered through the state departments of transportation in close coordination with FHWA's division offices (there is one in each state). Although ER is a federal program, the decision to seek ER funding is made by the state, not by the federal government. Most observers see the close and ongoing relationship between the FHWA's staff at the state level and their state counterparts as facilitating a quick coordinated response to disasters.

The program is funded by an annual $100 million authorization from the highway trust fund and general fund appropriations that are provided by

Congress on a such sums as necessary basis. A number of issues have arisen in recent years:

- The scope of eligible activities funded by ER has grown via legislative or FHWA waivers of eligibility criteria or changes in definitions that have expanded the scope of ER projects, sometimes beyond repairing or restoring highways to pre-disaster condition.
- The $100 million annual authorization has been exceeded nearly every fiscal year, requiring appropriations that can lead to delay in funding permanent repairs.
- Congress has directed that in some cases ER fully fund projects, without the normal 10% or 20% state matching share, putting financial pressure on the federal side of disaster highway assistance.

State requests for ER funding are at times backlogged. In a deficit-reduction environment, it is questionable whether the ER program can continue to loosen eligibility restrictions and forgo the state match without increasing the backlog.

Chapter 5 - The prohibition of tolling of federal-aid highways dates back to the Federal Road Act of 1916 (39 Stat. 355). Subsequent legislation modified the prohibition to the point where now the only significant part of the federal-aid highway system under the toll prohibition is the Interstate Highway System, comprising approximately 47,000 miles of the roughly 1-million-mile federal-aid highway system. Congress, in approving the Federal-Aid Highway Act and Highway Revenue Act of 1956 (P.L. 84-621; 70 Stat. 374), rejected the use of tolls or user fees to finance construction in favor of creating a highway trust fund supported by dedicated fuel taxes. However, certain existing expressway segments that were incorporated into the Interstate Highway System already had tolls in 1956, and they are not covered by the tolling prohibition.

In recent years the revenues flowing into the highway trust fund have been insufficient to maintain even current levels of federal funding for highways. Political resistance to raising the federal fuels tax is high. The fuel taxes dedicated to the highway trust fund, currently 18.3 cents per gallon of gasoline and 24.3 cents per gallon of diesel fuel, were last raised in 1993.

Historically, interest in toll financing has increased during periods of constrained federal funding. Since the Interstate Highways make up nearly all federal-aid highway segments that are still under the tolling prohibition, advocates of expanded use of tolling focus their efforts on giving states more flexibility to impose tolls on the Interstates within their borders.

Chapter 6 – Affordable access to broadband telecommunications is increasingly viewed as vital to the country's economic growth as well as for improving state and local systems for traffic management, public safety, and educational goals. According to the Federal Communications Commission (FCC), the largest cost element for deploying broadband via fiber optic cable is the cost of placement, such as burying the fiber in the ground, rather than the cost of the fiber itself. Recent legislation introduced in both the U.S. Senate and House of Representatives would require the Secretary of Transportation to require states to install broadband conduit during construction for certain federally funded highway projects in compliance with standards developed by the Secretary, in coordination with FCC. Both the House and Senate bills would make conduit available to any requesting broadband service provider for a "charge not to exceed a cost-based rate." Both bills would affect only new construction or highway expansion projects that receive federal funding and would not, for example, affect projects limited to road resurfacing or general maintenance.

You requested that we examine proposed federal "dig once" policies that would require the deployment of broadband conduit in conjunction with federally funded highway construction projects as a way to decrease the costs of deploying fiber and eliminate the need for multiple excavations. This report presents information on (1) the advantages and disadvantages of dig once policies and (2) how the broadband deployment experiences of states and localities that have implemented dig once policies can inform the consideration of a federal dig once policy.

Chapter 7 – In 2007, the Federal Highway Administration of the Department of Transportation (DOT) completed a rulemaking to revise the Manual of Uniform Traffic Control Devices (MUTCD) standard for night-time visibility (retroreflectivity) of street signs. The new standard set a minimum measured value for the retroreflectivity of street signs and required state and local agencies to adopt a method to maintain the retroreflectivity of their signs. Communities are required to comply with this standard by 2018.

In 2010, several press reports conflated this new standard with a 2009 MUTCD revised street sign standard—one having to do with the lettering style of street sign names, which had no compliance deadline—and became controversial, as the press reports made it appear that the federal government was requiring communities to replace street signs just to change their lettering style. This issue has come to the attention of Congress. In 2011 the DOT proposed to amend the target compliance date for the retroreflectivity standard (and several other MUTCD standards) to alleviate possible financial burdens the deadlines may create for highway agencies. Agencies will still be required to comply with the retroreflectivity standard. This report answers a number of questions that are frequently asked about this issue.

Chapter 8 - The federal government has provided aid for roads and highways since the establishment of the United States in 1789. This report comprises a brief history of such aid, detailing some precedent setters and more recent funding through the Highway Trust Fund, which was created in 1956.

In: Federal Programs and Policies for Highways   ISBN: 978-1-62257-755-2
Editors: E.D. Campbell and E.Sanchez   © 2013 Nova Science Publishers, Inc.

Chapter 1

THE FEDERAL EXCISE TAX ON GASOLINE AND THE HIGHWAY TRUST FUND: A SHORT HISTORY[*]

James M. Bickley

SUMMARY

Excise taxes have long been a part of our country's revenue history. In the field of gasoline taxation, the states led the way with Oregon enacting the first tax on motor fuels in 1919. By 1932, all states and the District of Columbia had followed suit with tax rates that ranged between two and seven cents per gallon.

The federal government first imposed its excise tax on gasoline at a one-cent per gallon rate in 1932. The gas tax was enacted to correct a federal budgetary imbalance. It continued to support general revenue during World War II and the Korean War.

Economists know the gasoline excise tax as a "manufacturer's excise tax" because the government imposes it at production (i.e., the producer, refiner, or importer) for efficiency in collection. Particularly in the short run, when the demand for gasoline is relatively inelastic, economists recognize that any increase in the gasoline tax ultimately falls on the consumer.

---

[*] This is an edited, reformatted and augmented version of a Congressional Research Service publication, CRS Report for Congress RL30304, from www.crs.gov, prepared for Members and Committees of Congress, dated March 9, 2012.

The Highway Revenue Act of 1956 established the federal Highway Trust Fund (HTF) for the direct purpose of funding the construction of an interstate highway system, and aiding in the finance of primary, secondary, and urban routes. Each time Congress has extended the Highway Trust Fund it has also extended the federal excise tax on gasoline.

For FY2011, the Congressional Budget Office estimated that revenues and interest credited to the Highway Trust Fund will total $36.9 billion, which will be divided into the Highway Account ($31.8 billion) and the Mass Transit Account ($5.1 billion).

CBO also estimated that the fund's three primary revenue sources and their yields will be the gasoline tax ($24.0 billion), the diesel tax ($8.7 billion), and the tax on trucks and trailers ($2.2 billion). On September 16, 2011, President Obama signed H.R. 2887, Surface and Air Transportation Programs Extension Act of 2011 (P.L. 112-30), which extended, through March 31, 2012, current surface transportation programs and the motor fuel, heavy truck, and truck tire taxes that support the HTF.

On November 9, 2011, the Senate Environment and Public Works Committee marked up and reported favorable on the highway provisions of S. 1813, the Moving Ahead for Progress in the 21st Century Act (MAP-21). S. 1813 is a two-year reauthorization bill for FY2012-FY2013 that basically funds the Federal-Aid Highway Program at the baseline level, adjusted for inflation.

This bill would also make substantial changes to the structure, formulas, and funding distribution of the federal highway program. As of February 7, 2012, all committees of jurisdiction had marked up their titles. On March 1, 2012, these titles were folded into S.Amdt. 1761 to S. 1813.

On March 5, 2012, in response to a request from Senate Majority Leader Harry Reid, the Congressional Budget Office (CBO) issued estimates for S. 1813, MAP-21, with amendment. CBO estimated that implementing the bill would have discretionary costs of $47.0 billion over the FY2012-FY2017 period.

In addition, CBO estimated that implementing the provisions of the bill for the remainder of FY2012 and for FY2013 would result in an end-of-year balance in 2013 of approximately $2 billion in the highway account of the HTF and about $3 billion in the transit account of the HTF.

On April 1, 2012, current surface transportation programs are scheduled to expire, and taxes that support the Highway Trust Fund are scheduled to expire or decline. The primary revenue source for the HTF, the gasoline tax, will decline from 18.4 cents per gallon to 4.3 cents per gallon.

INTRODUCTION

Although excise taxes have long been a source of federal tax revenue, the federal manufacturers excise tax on gasoline was first incorporated into the federal tax structure by the Revenue Act of 1932, which became law on June 6, 1932.[1] A manufacturer's excise tax is one that is collected at the level of production. A tax imposed at the production or importation level provides ease in administration and revenue collection.[2]

Prior to the 1932 act, there had been a reluctance on the part of federal officials and Congress to impose this tax at the federal level. Instead, they preferred to relinquish this revenue source to the states to help them finance their revenue needs. Oregon was the first state to levy a gasoline tax in 1919. As of January 1932, all of the states and the District of Columbia had enacted legislation imposing a tax on gasoline with rates that ranged from two to seven cents per gallon.

However, during the severe depression of the 1930s, federal revenues were sharply reduced and higher expenditures were made for relief and public works programs. As a result, the Secretary of the Treasury, in his annual report for FY1931, reported that the federal government had incurred a budgetary deficit of some $903 million that year. This marked the first year in more than a decade when federal receipts failed to exceed federal expenditures and produce a budgetary surplus. Moreover, the Secretary of the Treasury estimated then that even higher deficits were anticipated in the years immediately following: $2.1 billion in FY1932, and $1.4 billion in FY1933.

GASOLINE EXCISE TAX FOR DEFICIT REDUCTION—1932

To correct this budgetary imbalance, the Secretary of the Treasury submitted comprehensive tax-raising and expenditure-reduction proposals for congressional action. Among the tax recommendations were those for legislation increasing individual and corporation income, estate and gift, excise, and other taxes. Included in the excise tax proposals was the request for a new federal manufacturer's excise tax on gasoline, to be levied at the rate of one cent per gallon and scheduled to end in 1934. It was estimated that adoption of such a tax would yield the U.S. Treasury approximately $165 million in revenues during FY1933.

The House of Representatives, in its consideration of and action on these revenue-raising proposals, initially refused to impose a new federal tax on gasoline. The Senate amended the House-passed bill, however, authorizing a gasoline tax at the rate of one cent per gallon. Congress retained the tax in the final version of the bill approved by the House and Senate conference committee and signed into law.

As approved, Section 617(a) of the Revenue Act of 1932[3] imposed a federal tax on gasoline sold by a producer or importer at the rate of one cent per gallon. Under Section 617(c) of this legislation, the term "producer" included a "refiner, compounder, or blender, and a dealer selling gasoline exclusively to producers of gasoline, as well as a producer." Gasoline was defined to include gasoline, benzyl, and any other liquids used primarily as a fuel to propel motor vehicles, motor boats, or airplanes. Section 629 of this act made this tax effective on June 21, 1932, for a temporary period, with provision for its end just over a year later on June 30, 1933. The *Annual Report of the Commissioner of Internal Revenue* for FY1933 reported that the federal government derived $124.9 million from the excise tax on gasoline. Thus, the gasoline tax represented 7.7% of the total Internal Revenue collection of $1.62 billion derived from all sources during FY1933.

Shortly before the tax was scheduled to expire, Congress approved two bills that extended this tax for an additional year and increased its rate. Under P.L. 73 approved by the 73rd Congress,[4] Congress extended this tax until June 30, 1934. The National Industrial Recovery Act,[5] signed into law on the same day, included provisions governing the rate of this tax. Section 211(a) of this act authorized the increase in federal gasoline tax from one cent to 1.5 cents per gallon, effective June 17, 1933. Section 217(b) provided for this tax to be reduced to one cent per gallon on the first day of the calendar year following the date proclaimed by the President when either of the following occurred: (1) the close of the first fiscal year ending after 1933 when total federal receipts exceeded total federal expenditures, or (2) the repeal of the 18th amendment to the Constitution, establishing national prohibition (repeal would bring in additional revenues to the U.S. Treasury from alcohol taxes).

Subsequently, President Franklin D. Roosevelt proclaimed repeal of the 18th amendment to the Constitution on December 5, 1933. Therefore, under authority of Section 217(b) of the National Industrial Recovery Act, the federal gasoline tax reverted to its former rate of one cent per gallon on January 1, 1934. Section 603 of the Revenue Act of 1934,[6] approved in the spring of 1934, continued this tax at the rate of one cent per gallon beyond its scheduled expiration date of June 30, 1934.

NATIONAL DEFENSE REQUIREMENTS

The one-cent rate was maintained until just before the United States entered World War II, when, as a result of increased national defense requirements, Congress again took action increasing this tax. Section 210 of the Revenue Act of 1940[7] authorized an increase to 1.5 cents per gallon for the five-year period beginning on July 1, 1940, and continuing through June 30, 1945, as part of a defense tax. The following year, under Section 521(a)(20) of the Revenue Act of 1941,[8] this rate was made permanent by elimination of the June 30, 1945, expiration date that had been specified in the Revenue Act of 1940.

The 1.5-cent per gallon rate continued for more than a decade until the outbreak of the Korean War, when Congress increased the rate to two cents per gallon under authority of Section 489 of the Revenue Act of 1951.[9] This rate became effective on November 1, 1951, and Congress authorized it to continue until March 31, 1954. After this date, Congress scheduled the rate to be reduced to its former rate of 1.5 cents per gallon. Before this reduction took place, Congress passed the Excise Tax Reduction Act of 1954,[10] and under Section 601(a)(6) of this legislation, the two-cent per gallon rate was extended for an additional year—until March 31, 1955. During the next two years Congress passed legislation granting one-year extensions of the two-cent per gallon tax on gasoline by approval of the Tax Rate Extension Act of 1955[11] (Section 3(a)(3)) and the Tax Rate Extension Act of 1956[12] (Section 3(a)(3)), which continued the rate first to March 31, 1956, and then to March 31, 1957.

P.L. 466, approved by the 84th Congress,[13] provided that the Treasury Department refund those taxes paid on gasoline used on farms for farming purposes purchased after December 31, 1955.

HIGHWAY TRUST FUND

The Federal Aid Highway Act of 1956[14] provided for a significant expansion in the federal-aid highway program and authorized federal funding over a longer period to permit long-range planning. It was considered necessary to authorize the entire interstate highway program to assure orderly planning and completion of this network of highways throughout the United States as efficiently and as economically as possible. Consequently, this act authorized appropriations for the 13-year period from FY1957 through

FY1969 for this highway system. To make the federal aid highway program self-financing, the Highway Revenue Act of 1956[15] was incorporated as Title II of this legislation and imposed new taxes and increased others levied on highway users who directly benefitted from this program.

Section 205 of this Highway Revenue Act authorized an increase in the federal gasoline tax from two to three cents per gallon for the 16-year period from July 1, 1956, through June 30, 1972. After that, the Congress scheduled the tax to be reduced to 1.5 cents per gallon.

Section 209 of this act authorized the creation of the Highway Trust Fund, to which there was to be appropriated from the General Fund of the Treasury certain percentages of receipts derived from highway-user taxes: gasoline, diesel and special motor fuel, tread rubber, tires and inner tubes, trucks, buses, etc. One hundred percent of the federal gasoline tax receipts were transferred to the Highway Trust Fund.

It was argued that transferring such taxes to the Highway Trust Fund was necessary to cover anticipated expenditures to be made under the federal aid highway program for the 16-year period from FY1957 through FY1972. H.Rept. 2022 (84th Congress), issued on this legislation, estimated that highway-user taxes would yield some $38.5 billion in revenues for this trust fund during this 16-year period—enough to cover anticipated expenditures of approximately $37.3 billion (during this same period) for the federal aid highway program.

This legislation also arranged for refunding a certain portion of federal gasoline taxes paid that were used for non-highway purposes or by local transit systems.

Since enactment of this legislation, Congress has continued to pass laws extending the life of the Highway Trust Fund and extending and increasing the rates imposed on gasoline.

Under Section 201(a) of the Federal Aid Highway Act of 1959,[16] the federal gasoline tax was increased from three to four cents per gallon, a change that was to be in effect from October 1, 1959, through June 30, 1961.

Under Section 201(b) of the Federal Aid Highway Act of 1961,[17] this four-cent rate was extended beyond June 30, 1961. The scheduled reduction to 1.5 cents per gallon, which the Highway Revenue Act of 1956 had authorized to take place on July 1, 1972, was deferred until October 1, 1972.

Following the 1961 act, the next law affecting the federal gasoline tax was the Federal-Aid Highway Act of 1970.[18] Under Section 303(a)(6) of this act, the scheduled reduction in the rate of this tax to 1.5 cents per gallon was deferred from September 30, 1972, to September 30, 1977.

Again in 1976, an extension of excise tax rates without the scheduled rate reductions allocated to the Highway Trust Fund was provided in Title III of the Federal Aid Highway Act of 1976.[19] The Interstate Highway System was obviously not going to be completed in 1977 (it was estimated in 1976 that it might be completed in 1988). Lack of time to study and report to Congress on modifications to the Highway Trust Fund led to the two-year extension. Congress was concerned that without this legislation funding would be interrupted. Thus, Congress delayed decision-making until it could gather additional information.

Two years later, Congress had not yet decided on modifications to the trust fund and its related taxes. The Ways and Means Committee accepted the recommendation of the Public Works Committee and approved an extension of the trust fund and the taxes payable to the fund. This five-year extension through September 30, 1984, became part of the Surface Transportation Assistance Act of 1978.[20]

Congress gathered extensive information on highway finance and related taxes in 1982. Two major studies were submitted to Congress. The first was a cost allocation study done by the Department of Transportation in May 1982. The second was a study of the excise tax structure that the Department of the Treasury provided to Congress in December 1982. Further, Congress held more than a dozen hearings before the passage of the Surface Transportation Assistance Act of 1982.[21]

The act contains what is commonly called the 4R Program: interstate reconstruction, resurfacing, restoration, and rehabilitation. The completion and selective expansion of the Interstate Highway System remained the primary goals under the bill.

Congress raised the gasoline excise tax from its previous level of four cents per gallon to nine cents per gallon. With this increase, Congress eliminated some highway user charges while increasing others. The act also provided that one cent of the five-cent increase in the motor fuel taxes was to be allocated for mass transit purposes. The bill set up a special Mass Transit Account for expenditures made under the Urban Mass Transportation Act of 1964. In 1986, in response to concerns about the cost for cleanup of leaking underground storage tanks containing petroleum products, Congress established the Leaking Underground Storage Tank Trust Fund.[22] This fund received revenues of 0.1 cent per gallon on the sale or use of gasoline (first effective January 1, 1987). Congress scheduled the tax to expire on the earlier of December 31, 1991, or the last day of the month in which the Secretary of the Treasury estimated that net revenues in the fund were at least $500 million.

This additional tax ended after August 31, 1990, because the Leaking Underground Storage Tank Trust Fund had reached its net revenue target for cancellation.[23]

The Surface Transportation and Uniform Relocation Assistance Act of 1987[24] extended the highway-related excise taxes (including the tax on gasoline) through September 30, 1993.

GASOLINE EXCISE TAX FOR DEFICIT REDUCTION

Under provisions of the Omnibus Budget Reconciliation Act of 1990 (OBRA90),[25] the tax rate on highway and motorboat fuels was increased by five cents per gallon. Thus, the tax increased from nine to 14 cents per gallon of gasoline. Half of the increase in revenues from the gasoline tax imposed on highway use vehicles was dedicated as additional funding for the Highway Trust Fund.

The remaining half of revenues was deposited in the General Fund and dedicated for federal deficit reduction. Of the 2.5-cent increase dedicated to the Highway Trust Fund, 0.5 cents were dedicated to the Mass Transit Account in that trust fund. Thus, Congress raised the Mass Transit Account funding from one cent to 1.5 cents. OBRA90 also reinstated the Leaking Underground Storage Tank Trust Fund (LUST). The LUST tax recommenced at the same 0.1- cent-per-gallon tax rate.[26] The 14-cent tax rate was scheduled to expire on September 30, 1995, while the LUST tax was scheduled to terminate three months later on December 31, 1995.

The conventional view that had held since the establishment of the Highway Trust Fund, which was that the gasoline tax was a user tax, was challenged. With the passage of OBRA90, the gasoline tax returned to the role it served prior to 1957: a General Fund revenue source, at least in part.

The following year Congress passed the Intermodal Surface Transportation Efficiency Act (ISTEA) of 1991.[27] The revenue title is the Surface Transportation Revenue Act of 1991. This act extended the highway-related excise taxes (including the tax on gasoline in Section 8002(a)(3)) for four years.

Hence, this law extended the tax on gasoline (without an increase in tax rate) through September 30, 1999. In addition, under provisions of the act, states were permitted to spend their Highway Trust Fund grants on a broader range of alternative transportation modes and related infrastructure needs. This was done in response to the argument that highway users benefit from expenditures on mass transit and other transportation modes because the availability of these travel alternatives alleviates congestion on existing highways, which in turn reduces the need to build additional roadways.

Also included in provisions of ISTEA was the establishment of a new trust fund known as the National Recreational Trails Trust Fund. This fund receives tax transfers from the Highway Trust Fund that represent tax receipts (imposed on gasoline, diesel, and special motor fuels) collected from *non-highway* recreational fuel use.

Examples of recreational fuels are those used in vehicles on recreational trails or back-country terrain, and non-business fuel used in outdoor recreational equipment, such as camp stoves.

Once again, the gasoline excise tax was changed under provisions of the Omnibus Budget Reconciliation Act of 1993 (OBRA93, Section 13241(a)).[28] Under provisions of OBRA93, the additional 2.5-cent gasoline tax dedicated for deficit reduction was transferred to the Highway Trust Fund beginning October 1, 1995. This additional 2.5-cent tax rate was extended from October 1, 1995, to September 30, 1999. The highway portion of the fund receives two cents, while the Mass Transit Account is credited with 0.5 cent of the increased funding. In addition, OBRA93 provided for a permanent, additional 4.3 cents per gallon tax on gasoline starting on October 1, 1993. Thus, the combination of the 2.5-cents OBRA90 gasoline tax rate and the permanent 4.3-cent OBRA93 gasoline tax rate resulted in a total of 6.8 cents per gallon dedicated to deficit reduction purposes between October 1, 1993, and October 1, 1995. Revenues collected from this 6.8-cent portion of the tax were placed in the General Fund of the U.S. Treasury.

As previously related, provisions of OBRA90 terminated the LUST tax rate of 0.1 cent on December 31, 1995. Thus, the 18.3-cent federal gasoline excise tax rate was in effect from January 1, 1996, to October 1, 1997, before increasing to 18.4 cents with the reintroduction of the LUST tax. This 18.3-cent rate includes the permanent 4.3 cents initially dedicated to federal deficit reduction but which now goes to the Highway Trust Fund.

REVERSION FROM DEFICIT REDUCTION TO USER TAX STATUS

During the early months of 1996, the price of gasoline at the pump was rising and a renewed interest developed in federal gasoline excise taxes. Three principal views developed. The first view was that the 4.3 cents increase in federal excise taxes imposed under OBRA93 should be repealed. Proponents of repeal argued that the 4.3 cents repeal could lead to a similar reduction in gasoline pump prices. Two camps developed which supported retaining the tax. Some supporters of the tax expressed the view that while the 4.3-cent tax should be retained, the tax revenues should be returned to the Highway Trust Fund for long-term capital improvements. They argued for increased funding of the nation's highway infrastructure. Others expressed the view that the monies should continue to be collected and used for deficit reduction. This camp of supporters argued that the gasoline price increase was temporary and that over the long term prices would trend lower. Partially in response to this debate, the chairman of the House Ways and Means Committee, Representative Bill Archer, appointed a bi-partisan group to examine the tax treatment of each of the transportation modes with a goal of rationalizing the current myriad tax rules applying to the transportation sector.

Included in the Taxpayer Relief Act of 1997[29] was a provision that returns the General Fund portion of the tax back to the Highway Trust Fund. This provision, first added by a Senate amendment (and modified in conference), provides that the 4.3-cent tax is divided between the Highway Account (3.45 cents) and the Mass Transit Account (0.85 cent). The provision was effective on October 1, 1997. Thus, of the total 18.3 cents dedicated to the Highway Trust Fund, 15.44 cents goes to the Highway Account and 2.86 cents to the Mass Transit Account.[30] As a consequence, the disposition of revenues was altered by the act so that all revenues now accrue to the Highway Trust Fund and none are applied to deficit reduction. Consumers experienced no price change due to enactment of this provision since the federal tax rate on gasoline remained the same.

In addition, the Taxpayer Relief Act of 1997 reinstated the Leaking Underground Storage Tank Trust Fund excise tax, which had expired January 1, 1996.[31] The tax was reinstated at its prior tax rate of 0.1 cent per gallon on all types of motor fuels. The tax rate change was effective from October 1, 1997, through March 31, 2005.[32] The LUST excise tax was then extended for an additional seven months (through September 30, 2005).[33] Under a provision contained in the Energy Policy Act of 2005 the LUST tax is extended through September 30, 2011. The imposition of the gasoline tax is codified under IRC Section 4081.

Although the component of the federal gasoline tax formerly (but no longer) applied to deficit reduction continues without an expiration date, the 14 cents scheduled to expire on September 30, 1999, has been extended.

Congress not only extended the gasoline excise tax but also the other highway-related excise taxes. The House had proposed to extend the heavy truck tire tax until October 1, 2000, whereupon it would expire. However, in conference with the Senate, all the highway-related excise taxes were extended through September 30, 2005. The legislative vehicle for this extension was the Transportation Equity Act for the 21st Century[34] generally known as TEA-21. The revenue portion of this act (Title IX) was titled the Surface Transportation Revenue Act of 1998.

This act also provided that the Highway Trust Fund no longer earns interest on unspent balances (effective September 30, 1998). The balance of funds that exceed $8 billion in the Highway Account was canceled on October 1, 1998.

In addition, TEA-21 provided that the National Recreational Trails Trust Fund established under ISTEA be repealed. In the absence of an appropriation of funds, no revenues had been available for expenditure. The conference agreement noted that similar expenditure purposes are provided by authorized amounts from the Highway Trust Fund.

Beginning in the 108th Congress, a series of laws were passed extending the funding for Highway Trust Fund. These extensions during the 108th-111th Congresses are described in the *Appendix.*

EXTENSIONS IN THE 112TH CONGRESS

For FY2011, the Congressional Budget Office estimates that revenues and interest credited to the Highway Trust Fund will total $36.9 billion, which will be divided into the Highway Account ($31.8 billion) and the Mass Transit Account ($5.1 billion).[35] The three primary revenue sources will be the gasoline tax ($24.0 billion), the diesel tax ($8.7 billion), and the tax on trucks and trailers ($2.2 billion).[36] The tax on trucks and trailers will only finance highways.

On March 4, 2011, the *Surface Transportation Extension Act of 2011* (H.R. 662) became P.L. 112- 5. The law provided an extension of federal-aid highway, highway safety, motor carrier safety transit, and other programs funded out of the Highway Trust Fund through September 30, 2011.

On May 17, 2011, the Senate Finance Committee held a hearing on the "Highway Trust Fund and Paying for Highways." Joseph Kile, Assistant Director for Microeconomic Studies at CBO, testified:

The law that authorizes collection of taxes for and spending from the Highway Trust Fund is set to expire on September 30, 2011. Even if the provisions of that law are extended, the trust fund will be unable to meet its obligations in a timely manner by the summer or fall of 2012, CBO projects, unless transfers similar to those in the past are made, other sources of revenue are identified, or spending is reduced.[37]

Different options for financing highways were examined.[38]

On July 13, 2011, Representative Mica, chairman of the House Transportation and Infrastructure Committee, sent a letter to the U.S. Chamber of Commerce opposing the chamber's support for a gasoline tax increase.[39] In his letter, he stated:

> The reaction from National Chamber of Commerce representatives to the rollout of the Republican Surface Transportation Reauthorization outline was most disappointing and a potential setback to enacting a long term transportation reauthorization. During my years of service on the Transportation and Infrastructure Committee I have seen the National Chamber of Commerce evolve from an Association that would advocate strong infrastructure and responsible fiscal policy on behalf of its members to an organization whose primary purpose in the national infrastructure arena appears to be to lead the lobby for tax increases.[40]

Reportedly, Representative John Mica and Senator Barbara Boxer, chairwoman of the Senate Environment and Public Works Committee, have proposed long-term highway bills, which have substantial differences.[41]

On August 31, 2011, President Obama called on Congress to pass a clean extension of funding for the surface transportation law.[42] In response, Representative John L. Mica issued a press release that stated:

Republicans have offered positive and financially responsible alternatives to get these measures moving.

As Chairman of the House Transportation Committee, I will agree to one additional highway program extension, this being the eighth of the overdue transportation reauthorization.[43]

On September 13, 2011, the House approved H.R. 2887, *Surface Air Transportation Programs Act of 2011*, which extended through March 31, 2012, current surface transportation programs and the motor fuel, heavy truck, and truck tire taxes that support the Highway Trust Fund.[44] On September 15, 2011, the Senate approved H.R. 2887.[45] On September 16, 2011, President Obama signed H.R. 2887, P.L. 112-30.[46]

On October 31, 2011, Senator Amy Klobuchar introduced the *Rebuild America Jobs Act* (S. 1769). This bill included $50 billion for road, transit, rail, and aviation investments and $10 billion for the creation of a national infrastructure bank.[47] The bill proposed a 0.7% surcharge on households earning more than $1 million per year. On November 2, 2011, Senator Orrin Hatch introduced S. 1786, *Long-Term Surface Transportation Extension Act of 2011*, which would extend for two years Highway Trust Fund expenditure authority and highway-related taxes and rescind unspent federal funds to offset revenue losses.[48] On November 3, 2011, both S. 1769 and S. 1786 failed to obtain the 60 vote procedural threshold necessary for further consideration in the Senate.[49] On November 4, 2011, Senators Barbara Boxer and James Inhofe introduced a two-year reauthorization of U.S. surface transportation programs at current funding levels, *Moving Ahead for Progress in the 21st Century Act or (MAP-21)*.[50] This bill would also make substantial changes to the structure, formulas, and funding distribution of the federal highway program. On November 9, 2011, the Senate Environment and Public Works Committee marked up and reported favorable on the highway provisions of S. 1813, the *Moving Ahead for Progress in the 21st Century Act* (MAP-21). As of February 7, 2012, all committees of jurisdiction had marked up their titles. On March 1, 2012, these titles were folded into S.Amdt. 1761 to S. 1813. MAP-21 is currently beginning debated in the Senate.[51]

ISSUES

In economic theory, there are two principles often cited for determining how the burden of a tax ought to be distributed. The first is the ability-to-pay principle, which suggests that a tax ought to be positively related to an individual's economic welfare.

The second principle, the benefit principle, suggests the burden should relate to an individual's return from the government good or service funded by the tax. Currently, an excise tax on gasoline seems to most closely follow the benefits principle. In fact, the excise tax has commonly been referred to as a "user fee."

However, this is not the only economic rationale that could be forwarded in support of a gasoline tax. Some argue that gasoline taxes, and energy taxes, more generally, can be imposed to influence behavior, specifically as a mechanism to reduce, or internalize the costs of, social and environmental externalities such as congestion and pollution.[52]

Table 1. Summary of Changes in the Rate of the Federal Manufacturers' Excise Tax on Gasoline

Rate of Tax (in cents per gallon)	Period to Which Applicable
1	June 21, 1932, to June 16, 1933
1.5	June 17, 1933, to December 31, 1933
1	January 1, 1934, to June 30, 1940
1.5	July 1, 1940, to October 31, 1951
2	November 1, 1951, to June 30, 1956
3	July 1, 1956, to September 30, 1959
4	October 1, 1959, to March 31, 1983
9	April 1, 1983, to December 31, 1986
9.1	January 1, 1987, to August 31, 1990[a]
9	September 1, 1990, to November 30, 1990
14.1	December 1, 1990, to September 30, 1993
18.4	October 1, 1993, to December 31, 1995[b]
18.3	January 1, 1996,[c] to September 30, 1997
18.4	October 1, 1997,[d] to March 31, 2012
4.3	April 1, 2012, and thereafter

Source: Prepared by the Congressional Research Service.

[a] This act provided that the 0.1-cent per gallon tax will terminate on the earlier of December 31, 1991, or when the Secretary of the Treasury determines that taxes equivalent to at least $500 million in net revenues are in the Trust Fund. This additional tax terminated after August 31, 1990, because the LUST Trust Fund had reached its net revenue target for termination. (Internal Revenue Service Announcement 90-82, released June 27, 1990.)

[b] Beginning on October 1, 1995, the revenues collected from the 2.5-cent "deficit reduction" rate are to be credited to the account of the Highway Trust Fund. Thus, while the gasoline excise tax rate holds constant at 18.4 cents, the distribution of amounts collected from the gasoline excise tax changes. The Highway Trust Fund will receive increased revenues as the rate credited to that fund increases from 11.5 to 14 cents. At this same time, the amount credited to the General Fund decreases from 6.8 to 4.3 cents.

[c] Pursuant to provisions of OBRA90, the LUST tax terminated on December 31, 1995.

[d] Beginning on October 1, 1997, the Taxpayer Relief Act of 1997 provides that amounts previously dedicated for deficit reduction be redirected to the Highway Trust Fund. Additionally, the LUST tax which had terminated on December 31, 1996, was re-authorized for the period October 1, 1997, through March 31, 2005. A seven month extension (P.L. 109-6) extends the tax until October 2005. Passage of the Energy Policy Act of 2005 extended the LUST financing tax rate through September 30, 2011. On September 16, 2011, President Obama signed H.R. 2887, Surface and Air Transportation Programs Extension Act of 2011(P.L. 112- 30), which extended the tax until March 31, 2012.

The economic benefits derived from the expenditure of funds for transportation infrastructure, while important to the analysis, are distinct from the associated costs and benefits related to the method of raising the necessary revenues.

Particularly in the short run, when the demand for gasoline is relatively inelastic, economists recognize any increase in the gasoline tax is generally passed forward to consumers in the form of higher prices. As consumers modify their behaviors to respond to the increase in price (depending upon the magnitude), economic theory would predict consumers would purchase less gasoline, all else being equal. As a result, producers and retailers may not be able to pass on the entire magnitude of the tax to consumers. Although consumers would likely bear the majority of the excise tax increase on gasoline, producers may have lower net revenues and, thus, share some portion of the burden. See *Table 1* for a complete summary of the gasoline tax rate changes. On March 5, 2012, in response to a request from Senate Majority Leader Harry Reid, the Congressional Budget Office (CBO) issued estimates for S. 1813, MAP-21, with S.Amdt. 1761. CBO estimated that implementing the bill would have discretionary costs of $47.0 billion over the FY2012-FY2017 period. In addition, CBO estimated that implementing the provisions of the bill for the remainder of FY2012 and for FY2013 would result in an end-of-year balance in 2013 of approximately $2 billion in the highway account of the Highway Trust Fund and about $3 billion in the transit account of the Highway Trust Fund.[53] On April 1, 2012, current surface transportation programs are scheduled to expire and taxes that support the Highway Trust Fund are scheduled to expire or decline. The primary revenue source for the Highway Trust Fund, the gasoline tax, will decline from 18.4 cents per gallon to 4.3 cents per gallon.

APPENDIX. EXTENSIONS OF FUNDING FOR THE HIGHWAYS TRUST FUND: 108TH-111TH CONGRESSES

Extensions in the 108th Congress

Lawmakers first enacted the Surface Transportation Extension Act of 2003 (P.L. 108-88), which was a short-term extension of the highway, highway safety, motor carrier safety, transit, and other programs funded out of the Highway Trust Fund. The five-month extension was signed into law by

President Bush September 30, 2003. Four additional short-term extensions were enacted after the expiration of this initial extension. The Surface Transportation Extension Act of 2004 became P.L. 108-202 in February 2004. Part III of the Surface Transportation Extension Act of 2004, P.L. 108-263, was enacted in June 2004, and Part IV of the act, P.L. 108-280, became law at the end of July 2004. The Surface Transportation Extension Act of 2004, Part V became P.L. 108-310 and provided extensions through May 31, 2005, for those programs authorized by the Transportation Equity Act for the 21st Century (TEA-21). This last extension provided $31.8 billion in contract authority, of which $2.7 billion was for FY2004 and $29.1 billion was available for the eight-month period from October 1, 2004, through May 31, 2005. Under provisions of the Transportation Equity Act for the 21st Century, expenditures from the trust fund would have ceased if Congress had failed to approve these short-term extensions.[54] The revenue sources for the Highway Trust Fund include six different excise taxes, which are taxes on the highway motor fuels, gasoline, diesel fuel, and kerosene; a retail sales tax on heavy highway vehicles; a manufacturers' excise tax on heavy vehicle tires;[55] and an annual use tax on heavy vehicles. These excises were not affected by the temporary extensions, since under the law at that time the excise taxes were not scheduled for expiration until September 30, 2005.

Extensions in the 109th Congress

The 109th Congress initially had until Memorial Day to complete work on the new highway bill. That extension included language that provided for the 2.5 cents per gallon tax on ethanol to be deposited into the Highway Trust Fund for one year. Those monies had previously been deposited into the general fund. That change was estimated to generate $940 million in new revenue for the Highway Trust Fund. Also included was a one-year extension of the budgetary fire walls that tie gas tax revenue to highway and transit programs, while at the same time waiving for one year the Byrd self-solvency test for the trust fund and releasing the $716 million the Federal Highway Administration was holding onto as a result of the trust funds failure of that test. Further, the extension "also included a new 'supplemental minimum guarantee' program that was designed to ensure that all states continue to receive their 90.5% minimum guaranteed rate of return on fuel taxes sent to the Highway Trust Fund."[56] Again in the 109th Congress, it was necessary to pass a number of extensions so that the Highway Trust Fund could continue operations until enactment of a longer term re-authorizing measure. Accordingly, these extensions were known as the Surface Transportation Extension Acts of 2005.[57] Just prior to the summer recess, Congress sent legislation (H.R. 3) to the President which extended trust fund expenditures through FY2009 and continued the highway related taxes through FY2011. The legislation also included provisions aimed at stopping fuel fraud, provided tax-exempt financing authority to finance highway projects and rail-truck transfer facilities, and modified a number of excise taxes (both highway and non-highway related). President Bush signed the Safe, Accountable, Flexible, Efficient Transportation Equity Act: A Legacy for Users (SAFETEA-LU) (the "Highway Act") into law on August 10, 2005. The act extended for six years the Highway Trust Fund excise taxes due to expire in 2005 until 2011. All of the excise taxes, including the federal excise tax on gasoline, were continued at the prior tax rates. The act established the Motor Fuel Tax Enforcement Advisory Commission, which was scheduled to terminate on September 30, 2009. In other legislation, the Energy Policy Act of 2005 extended the Leaking Underground Storage Tank (LUST) Trust Fund financing rate for the same six-year period that the highway excise taxes were extended. Thus, the LUST tax will expire after September 30, 2011.

Extensions in the 110th Congress

At the time of passage of SAFETEA-LU, tax changes, the unexpended balance in the trust fund and economic growth were expected to provide sufficient financing for the Highway Trust Fund. But shortfalls developed which required general fund contributions.[58] On September 15, 2008, P.L. 110-318, *To Amend the Internal Revenue Code of 1986 to Restore the Highway Trust Fund Balance*, was passed. This law transferred $8.017 billion from the U.S. Treasury to the Highway Trust Fund, which provided financing through the end of FY2008.

Extensions in the 111th Congress

According to the Congressional Budget Office,

In 2010, the Hiring Incentives to Restore Employment Act (P.L. 111-147) authorized the most recent transfer from the general fund and the resumption of interest credits to the trust fund. That law also shifted certain refunds for tax-exempt use of motor fuels, such as fuel consumed by state and local governments, from being paid out of the Highway Trust Fund tobeing paid out of the general fund, also boosting trust fund balances. Because of the infusion of general revenues, at the end of 2010, the account balances were positive.[59]

On December 22, 2010, the *Continuing Appropriations and Surface Transportation Extension Act, 2011* (H.R. 3082) became P.L. 111-322. This law extended SAFETEA-LU authorization of appropriations out of the Highway Trust Fund through March 4, 2011.

End Notes

[1] The author updated this report, which was previously written by Pamela J. Jackson.
[2] For an analysis of the economic effects of a change in the amount of the gasoline tax, see CRS Report R40808, The Role of Federal Gasoline Excise Taxes in Public Policy, by Robert Pirog.
[3] Revenue Act of 1932, P.L. 154, 72nd Congress, approved June 6, 1932.
[4] Act to Extend the Gasoline Tax for One Year, to Modify Postage Rates on Mail Matter and for other Purposes, P.L. 73, 73rd Congress, approved June 16, 1933.
[5] National Industrial Recovery Act, P.L. 67, 73rd Congress, approved June 16, 1933.
[6] Revenue Act of 1934, P.L. 216, 73rd Congress, approved May 10, 1934.
[7] Revenue Act of 1940, P.L. 656, 76th Congress, approved June 25, 1940.
[8] Revenue Act of 1941, P.L. 250, 77th Congress, approved September 20, 1941.
[9] Revenue Act of 1951, P.L. 183, 82d Congress, approved October 20, 1951.
[10] Excise Tax Reduction Act of 1954, P.L. 324, 83rd Congress, approved March 31, 1954.
[11] Tax Rate Extension Act of 1955, P.L. 18, 84th Congress, approved March 30, 1955.
[12] Tax Rate Extension Act of 1956, P.L. 458, 84th Congress, approved March 29, 1956.
[13] Act to Amend the Internal Revenue Code of 1954 to Relieve Farmers from Excise Taxes in the Case of Gasoline and Special Fuels Used on Farms for Farming Purposes, P.L. 266, 84th Congress, approved April 1 2, 1956.
[14] Federal-Aid Highway and Highway Revenue Act of 1956, P.L. 627, 84th Congress, approved June 29, 1956.
[15] Ibid.
[16] Federal-Aid Highway Act of 1959, P.L. 86-342, approved September 21, 1959.
[17] Federal-Aid Highway Act of 1961, P.L. 87-61, approved June 29, 1961.
[18] Federal-Aid Highway Act of 1970, P.L. 91-605, approved December 31, 1970.
[19] Federal-Aid Highway Act of 1976, P.L. 94-280, approved May 5, 1976.
[20] Surface Transportation Assistance Act of 1978, P.L. 95-599, approved November 6, 1978.
[21] Surface Transportation Assistance Act of 1982, P.L. 97-424, approved January 6, 1983.
[22] Superfund Revenue Act of 1986, P.L. 99-499, approved October 17, 1986.
[23] Internal Revenue Service Announcement 90-82, released June 27, 1990.

[24] Surface Transportation and Uniform Relocation Assistance Act of 1987, P.L. 100-17, approved April 2, 1987.

[25] Omnibus Budget Reconciliation Act of 1990, P.L. 101-508, approved November 5, 1990.

[26] This act also instituted a new 2.5-cent per gallon tax on fuels used in rail transportation effective on December 1, 1990. Rail transportation generally uses diesel fuel. All revenues from this new tax go to general fund revenues with the tax scheduled to expire on October 1, 1995.

[27] Intermodal Surface Transportation Efficiency Act (ISTEA) of 1991, P.L. 102-240, approved December 18, 1991.

[28] Omnibus Budget Reconciliation Act of 1993, P.L. 103-66, approved August 10, 1993.

[29] Taxpayer Relief Act of 1997, P.L. 105-34, approved August 5, 1997.

[30] A technical correction contained in the Transportation Equity Act for the 21st Century (discussed later in this report) provides that deposits are to be equal to 2.86 cents per gallon rather than the 2.85 cents provided in the 1997 Act.

[31] Ibid.

[32] For additional information and a discussion of the LUST tax, see CRS Report RS21201, Leaking Underground Storage Tanks (USTs): Prevention and Cleanup, by Mary Tiemann.

[33] Extension of the Leaking Underground Storage Tank Trust Fund Financing Rate, P.L. 109-6, approved March 31, 2005.

[34] Transportation Equity Act for the 21st Century, P.L. 105-178, approved June 9, 1998.

[35] Ibid., p. 4.

[36] Ibid.

[37] Ibid., p. 1.

[38] Nicola M. White, "Finance Committee Seeks Ways to Fund Transportation Infrastructure," Tax Notes, May 23, 2011, p. 797. For an examination of different possible revenue sources for surface transportation infrastructure, see CRS Report R41490, Surface Transportation Funding and Finance, by Robert S. Kirk and William J. Mallett.

[39] Adam Snider, "U.S. Chamber's Support for Gas Tax Hike Imperils Surface Transport Bill," Mica Says, Daily Tax Report, August 19, 2012, p. G3.

[40] Representative John L. Mica, letter to Thomas J. Donohue, President and CEO of the U.S. Chamber of Commerce, July 13, 2011.

[41] Keith Laing and Bernie Becker, "Gas Tax Issue Could Be Next Political Fight in Congress," The Hill, vol. 18, no. 118, August 10, 2011, p. 4.

[42] Michael M. Gleeson, "Obama Calls for Clean Extension of Highway, Aviation Authorization and Taxes," Tax Notes Today, September 1, 2011, pp. 1-2.

[43] John Mica, Statement on President's Transportation Remarks, Press Release, August 31, 2011, p. 1.

[44] Adam Snider, "House Passes Transportation Stopgap But Coburn Could Slow Senate Floor Action," Daily Report for Executives, September 14, 2011, p. A18.

[45] Adam Snider, "Senate OKs Transportation Policy Stopgap After Promise for Long-Term FAA Measure," Daily Report for Executives, September 16, 2011, p. A27.

[46] Adam Snider, "Obama Signs Highway, FAA Stopgap Bill, Avoiding Lapse in Aviation, Motor Fuel Taxes," Daily Report For Executives, September 19, 2011, p. G5.

[47] Christine Grimaldi, "Democrats' Infrastructure Bill with Surtax, GOP Alternative Fail to Advance in Senate," Daily Tax Report, November 4, 2011, p. G6.

[48] "Hatch Bill Would Extend Highway Trust Fund, Highway Taxes," Tax Notes Today, November 3, 2011, p.1.

[49] Christine Grimaldi, "Democrats' Infrastructure Bill With Surtax, GOP Alternative Fail To Advance in Senate," p. G6.

[50] "Senators Boxer, Inhofe Unveil Surface Transportation Reauthorization Bill," Daily Report for Executives, November 4, 2011, p. 1.

[51] CRS Report R42120, Surface Transportation Reauthorization Legislation in the 112th Congress: Major Provisions Pending in the Senate, coordinated by Robert S. Kirk, pp. 9-13.

[52] In economics, an externality arises when either the production or consumption of a good or service results in an indirect cost or benefit, which is not reflected in market prices.

[53] Congressional Budget Office, Letter to Honorable Harry Reid about cost estimates for S. 1813, March 5, 2012, p. 1.

[54] For an additional historical perspective on extension legislation, see CRS Report RS21621, Surface Transportation and Aviation Extension Legislation: A Historical Perspective, by John W. Fischer and Robert S. Kirk.

[55] The American Jobs Creation Act of 2004 (P.L. 108-357) replaced the tax on tires from one based on tire weight to a tax based on tire load capacity. This legislation also added definitions of "taxable tires," "bias ply tires," and "super single tires." Additional clarification of the definition for "super single tires" was provided with passage of the Energy Policy Act of 2005.

[56] Heather M. Rothman, "Highway Funding Extension Bill Cleared, With Provisions for AMT Relief, Expensing," Daily Tax Report, October 1, 2004, No. 190, p. G-11.

[57] Surface Transportation Extension Act of 2005, Part I, P.L. 109-14, approved May 31, 2005. Part II, P.L. 109-20, approved July 1, 2005. Part III, P.L. 109-35, approved July 20, 2005. Part IV, P.L. 109-37, approved July 22, 2005. Part V, P.L. 109-40, approved July 28, 2005. Part VI, P.L. 109-42, approved July 30, 2005.

[58] CRS Report R41490, Surface Transportation Funding and Finance, by Robert S. Kirk and William J. Mallett, p. 2.

[59] Congressional Budget Office, The Highway Trust Fund and Paying for Highways, Statement of Joseph Kile, Assistant Director for Microeconomic Studies, before the Senate Committee on Finance, May 17, 2011, p. 7.

In: Federal Programs and Policies for Highways   ISBN: 978-1-62257-755-2
Editors: E.D. Campbell and E.Sanchez © 2013 Nova Science Publishers, Inc.

Chapter 2

THE HIGHWAY TRUST FUND AND PAYING FOR HIGHWAYS. TESTIMONY OF JOSEPH KILE, ASSISTANT DIRECTOR FOR MICROECONOMIC STUDIES, CONGRESSIONAL BUDGET OFFICE, DELIVERED AT THE HEARING ON "FINANCING 21ST CENTURY INFRASTRUCTURE"[*]

NOTES

Unless otherwise noted, all years referred to are federal fiscal years, which run from October 1 to September 30.

Numbers in the text and tables may not add up to totals because of rounding.

---

[*] This is an edited, reformatted and augmented version of a testimony presented before the Senate Finance Committee, Hearing on "Financing 21st Century Infrastructure", dated May 17, 2011.

INTRODUCTION

Chairman Baucus, Senator Hatch, and Members of the Committee, thank you for the invitation to testify on issues related to the funding of highways. My testimony draws on several publications of the Congressional Budget Office (CBO) that discuss highways and other infrastructure related to transportation, water resources, and wastewater.[1] Although the testimony is focused on highways, the principles discussed here are relevant to all infrastructure that is financed by the public sector.

SUMMARY

This testimony reviews the status of the Highway Trust Fund and examines three questions facing the Congress:

- How much should the federal government spend on highways?
- How should the federal government direct the use of those funds?
- How should the federal government raise those funds?

Status of the Highway Trust Fund

The United States spends about $160 billion annually on highways, with about one-fourth of that total, or roughly $40 billion, coming from the federal government.

Federal highway spending is funded mainly through taxes on gasoline and other motor fuels that accrue to the Highway Trust Fund. In recent years, the Congress has spent more on highways than the revenues accruing to the fund for that purpose, and it has supplemented the trust fund's balance with money from the general fund of the Treasury.

The law that authorizes collection of taxes for and spending from the Highway Trust Fund is set to expire on September 30, 2011. Even if the provisions of that law are extended, the trust fund will be unable to meet its obligations in a timely manner by the summer or fall of 2012, CBO projects, unless transfers similar to those in the past are made, other sources of revenue are identified, or spending is reduced.

How Much Should the Federal Government Spend on Highways?

The Congress has a range of options for future spending on highways, and the one it selects will influence the amount and distribution of economic benefits from the nation's network of highways and roads. Those options include the following:

- Limit spending to the amount that is collected in current taxes on fuel and other transportation activities; doing so would result in spending that would be about $13 billion per year below the current amount.
- Maintain current capital spending, adjusted for inflation.
- Spend enough to maintain the current performance of the highway system; doing so would require about $14 billion per year more than current spending.
- Fund projects whose benefits exceed their costs; doing so would require even more spending than maintaining current services, up to about $50 billion more than current spending, depending on the degree to which benefits would be expected to exceed costs.

The additional spending needed to meet specific performance goals or to fund projects whose benefits exceed their costs would be less if highway users paid tolls that varied with congestion. Doing so would reduce demand for future spending by providing an incentive to use those roads less during congested periods. Although the size of that reduction is uncertain, the Federal Highway Administration (FHWA) estimates that the spending required to maintain current services or realize additional benefits from highways could be one-quarter to one-third less than current estimates if congestion pricing was widely adopted.

How Should the Federal Government Direct the Use of Highway Funds?

From the point of view of economic efficiency, the authority to make decisions about which highway projects to undertake is best placed with those who have the incentive and the information to weigh all of the costs and benefits of the decisions. Whether the federal government or state or local governments are more likely to make more efficient decisions about highway projects depends on who receives benefits from those decisions and who bears the costs.

The Congress currently directs resources for highway infrastructure through three mechanisms:

- About 80 percent of the money the federal government spends goes to grants to state governments under formulas that allocate funds for such purposes as construction, rehabilitation of existing roads, and safety programs. The remaining 20 percent goes to specific projects or purposes identified by the Congress or by the Secretary of Transportation.

- The federal government lends money to state and local governments and provides loan guarantees that reduce their cost of borrowing. Although that leverage allows more projects to be built today with a given amount of federal funds, the borrowed money ultimately must be repaid—either by state and local taxpayers or by highway users. The reduction in the cost to state and local governments imposes a cost on federal taxpayers, who bear the risk of default; that cost would otherwise be borne by the borrowers through the interest rates they would pay.

- The federal government also reduces the cost of borrowing for state and local governments by offering tax preferences for bonds they issue. Tax-exempt bonds use a well-established tax preference. However, they are not generally considered cost-effective because the federal revenues that are forgone may be significantly greater than the reduction in state and local borrowing costs. In recent years, the Congress has authorized tax credit bonds, which allow bondholders to claim a credit against their tax liability (or, in certain cases, to bond issuers, who can claim a credit payable by the Secretary of the Treasury). Such bonds can be a less expensive way for the federal government to reduce the cost of borrowing by state and local governments.

Some funding mechanisms concentrate decisionmaking authority with the federal government; others offer greater latitude for state and local governments. Currently, state and local governments choose most federally funded projects. However, concerns about that process have motivated proposals for a federal infrastructure bank that might use the results of cost–

benefit analyses to select projects. In addition, a federal infrastructure bank could lower the cost of borrowing by providing credit assistance and thus could attract private financing; however, it would impose the cost of such credit assistance on federal taxpayers.

How Should the Federal Government Raise Funds for Highways?

Funding for highway infrastructure ultimately comes either from highway users or from taxpayers, regardless of how the financing of a project is structured.

Taxes, tolls, and fees imposed on highway users now fund about half of highway spending by federal, state, and local governments; the rest comes from the Treasury's general fund and from similar state and local funds. Judging from estimates of the costs of highway use, a system that charged for the full cost of travel would have most if not all motorists paying substantially more than they do now—perhaps several times more, potentially providing more than sufficient revenue for spending on highways.

As with other decisions, concerns about fairness are important in determining where to find the required funds. For example, whether increased user charges would impose relatively greater burdens on low-income and rural users would depend on the structure of those charges.

Increasing the charges that users pay also could promote more efficient use of the highway system. Although taxes currently are charged for fuel, most of the costs of using a highway—including pavement damage, congestion, accidents, and noise— are tied more closely to the number of miles traveled than to the amount of fuel consumed. Fuel consumption depends not only on the number of miles traveled but also on fuel efficiency, which differs among vehicles and changes with driving conditions; therefore, charging highway users for the full costs of their use, or charging in proportion to the full costs, could not be accomplished solely through fuel taxes. Charging users according to costs would require a combination of fuel taxes and per-mile charges, sometimes called vehicle-miles traveled (VMT) taxes. Imposing such prices on system use would promote efficiency by encouraging motorists to use highways only when the benefits to them outweigh the full costs of that use. Alternatively, revenues could be raised from sources unrelated to transportation. That approach, however, would not promote efficient use of highways.

**Table 1. Estimated Revenues and Interest Credited
to the Highway Trust Fund, by Source, 2011**

	Highway	Mass Transit Account	Total	Share of Total Trust Fund Revenues and Interest(Percent)
Gasoline Tax	20.2	3.9	24.0	65
Diesel Tax	7.6	1.0	8.7	24
Tax on Trucks and Trailers	2.2	0	2.2	6
Use Tax on Certain Vehicles	1.0	0	1.0	3
Truck Tire Tax	0.4	0	0.4	1
Interest Credited	0.4	0.2	0.6	2
Total	*31.8*	*5.1*	*36.9*	*100*

Source: Congressional Budget Office.

THE HIGHWAY TRUST FUND

The federal government's surface transportation programs are financed mostly through the Highway Trust Fund, an accounting mechanism in the federal budget that comprises two separate accounts, one for highways and one for mass transit. The trust fund records specific cash inflows from revenues collected on excise taxes on the sale of motor fuels, trucks and trailers, and truck tires; taxes on the use of certain kinds of vehicles; and interest credited to the fund (see Table 1). In some years, the Congress has enacted laws to transfer money from the general fund of the Treasury to the Highway Trust Fund to ensure that the fund retains a positive balance. The Highway Trust Fund also records cash outflows for spending on designated highway and mass transit programs. (Some transit programs receive appropriations from the Treasury's general fund.) The largest component of spending, by far, is for the federal-aid highway program (see Table 2).

Excise taxes on motor fuels generate 89 percent of the Highway Trust Fund's revenues and interest, mostly from the tax of 18.3 cents per gallon on gasoline and ethanol-blended fuels. Under current law, most of that tax—14 cents per gallon—is set to expire on September 30, 2011. The remaining 4.3 cents per gallon will no longer be credited to the trust fund but will go to the Treasury's general fund. The gasoline tax is the source of about two-thirds of the fund's total revenues and interest. The second-largest source is the diesel fuel tax of 24.3 cents per gallon, which accounts for about one-quarter of the fund's revenues and interest. The balance comes from the other taxes and interest that are credited to the fund. Most of the revenue from fuel taxes is credited to the highway account of the trust fund, but 2.86 cents per gallon of all fuel taxes credited to the Highway Trust Fund goes to the mass transit account, which receives about 14 percent of the trust fund's revenues and interest.

Table 2. Components of the Highway Trust Fund, 2011
(Billions of dollars)

	Estimated Revenues and Interest[a]	Budget Authority and Obligation Limitations[b]	Estimated Outlays
Highway Trust Fund	36.9	52.7	44.3
Highway account	31.8	44.3	36.7
Federal-aid highway program	n.a.	43.0	35.4
Motor carrier safety program	n.a.	0.6	0.5
Highway traffic safety program	n.a.	0.7	0.7
Mass transit account	5.1	8.4	7.6

Source:Congressional Budget Office.

Note:n.a. = not applicable.

[a] Revenues are deposited in the highway and mass transit accounts but are not designated for specific purposes. Those designations come from budget authority as specified in legislation such as the Safe, Accountable, Flexible, Efficient Transportation Equity Act: A Legacy for Users.

[b] Obligation limitations enacted in appropriation acts limit the amount of budget authority available to most Highway Trust Fund programs. The amounts shown are the sum of obligation limitations and budget authority that is not subject to any such limitation.

Spending from the Highway Trust Fund is determined by authorization acts that provide budget authority for highway programs, mostly in the form of contract authority (the authority to incur obligations in advance of appropriations).[2] Annual spending from the fund is largely controlled by limitations on the amount of contract authority that can be obligated in a particular year, and such obligation limitations are customarily set in annual appropriation acts.[3]

The most recent authorization law to govern spending from the trust fund is the Safe, Accountable, Flexible, Efficient Transportation Equity Act: A Legacy for Users (often called SAFETEA-LU), which expired in 2009 but has since operated under a series of short-term extensions, the latest of which is set to expire on September 30, 2011. SAFETEA-LU provides specific amounts of contract authority and authorizes appropriations for some programs that are not funded through contract authority. It also specifies annual obligation limitations, which may be superseded each year by limitations set in appropriation acts.

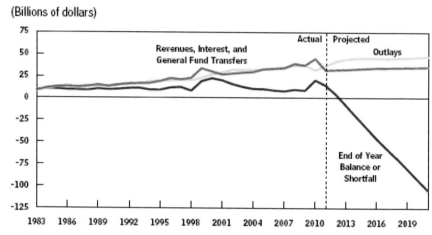

Source: Congressional Budget Office.

Note: Under current law, the Highway Trust Fund cannot incur negative balances. The negative balances shown above illustrate the projected inability of the fund to pay obligations as they are incurred by the states. If the Highway Trust Fund was unable to meet its obligations in a timely manner, spending on programs financed by the fund could continue more slowly, to keep pace with tax collections. The Department of Transportation has stated that if the fund faced a shortfall, it would ration the amounts it reimburses to states in order to maintain a positive balance in the fund.

Figure 1. Status of the Highway Account of the Highway Trust Fund.

History of the Highway Trust Fund's Revenues and Outlays

Highway Trust Fund balances once were stable, but over the past decade, the fund's receipts have fallen behind its expenditures. Balances in the highway account of the Highway Trust Fund were steady during the 1980s and the first half of the 1990s, in the vicinity of $10 billion (see Figure 1). The most recent increase in the gasoline tax occurred in 1993; after the Taxpayer Relief Act of 1997 redirected 4.3 cents of that tax from the general fund to the

Highway Trust Fund, the unexpended balance in the highway account began growing rapidly. Then, an agreement to spend down balances in the trust fund, which began with the enactment of the Transportation Equity Act for the 21st Century (known as TEA-21) in 1998, also eliminated the practice of crediting interest to the trust fund. Since 2001, outlays, which were boosted by TEA-21 and SAFETEA-LU, have generally exceeded revenues.

On several occasions since 2008, the Department of Transportation (DOT) has indicated that the trust fund would not meet its obligations on time without a transfer from the Treasury's general fund. Since then, the Congress has appropriated a total of $34.5 billion from the general fund to the Highway Trust Fund. In 2010, the Hiring Incentives to Restore Employment Act (Public Law 111-147) authorized the most recent transfer from the general fund and the resumption of interest credits to the trust fund. That law also shifted certain refunds for tax-exempt use of motor fuels, such as fuel consumed by state and local governments, from being paid out of the Highway Trust Fund to being paid out of the general fund, also boosting trust fund balances. Because of the infusion of general revenues, at the end of 2010, the account balances were positive: The highway account had $20.7 billion and the transit account had $8.9 billion.

Projections of the Highway Trust Fund's Revenues and Outlays

CBO estimates revenues and outlays independently to project what the trust fund's balances might be in the future. Revenues depend on the collection of various taxes. Under the rules that CBO follows in constructing its baseline revenue projections, the expiring excise taxes dedicated to the Highway Trust Fund are assumed to be extended beyond their scheduled expiration. Outlays depend on the obligation limitations set in appropriation acts as well as on the timing of spending for obligations that are incurred. For its projections, CBO assumes that policymakers will continue to control spending through such limitations. Furthermore, for the purpose of those projections, the agency assumes that appropriation acts will set obligation limitations equal to those enacted in the 2011 DOT appropriation act, adjusted for inflation.

If the current taxes are extended beyond their 2011 expiration date, CBO estimates, revenues and interest credited to the Highway Trust Fund will grow from $36.9 billion in 2011 to $40.9 billion in 2021. Over that period, the estimated rate of increase is projected to average a little more than 1 percent per year, which largely reflects expected growth in gasoline and diesel fuel consumption.

CBO bases its estimates of trust fund outlays for a given set of obligation limitations primarily on historical spending patterns, which reflect states' multiyear projects to plan and build roads, bridges, and other transportation infrastructure. Most obligations for the highway account involve capital projects on which money is spent over several years. (The federal-aid highway program, for example, typically spends about 25 percent of its budgetary resources in the year they are made available for spending; the rest is spent over the next several years.) Most of the highway account's existing obligations will therefore be met using tax revenues that have not yet been collected, because the obligations far exceed the amounts currently in the account. CBO estimates that at the end of 2011, the balance in the highway account will be $14.8 billion but outstanding obligations will total about $75 billion (by comparison, at the end of 2007, outstanding obligations totaled about $45 billion).

Even if lawmakers set obligation limitations to increase at the rate of inflation, CBO estimates, outlays from the highway account would rise from $32.0 billion in 2010 to $36.7 billion in 2011 and subsequently to $41.9 billion in 2012. That increase is largely attributable to the fact that general funds appropriated under the American Recovery and Reinvestment Act of 2009 (ARRA, P.L.111-5) temporarily displaced some spending from the highway account in 2009 and 2010. States had greater incentive to use ARRA funds than highway account funds because they were required to obligate ARRA funds more quickly than highway account funds and because they did not need to contribute any state or local resources to projects using ARRA funds, as is the case for projects funded from the highway account. Now that funds from ARRA have mostly been spent, CBO expects that state governments will spend the unused balances from appropriations for regular programs of the trust fund. In addition, CBO anticipates that about $2 billion from the highway account will be transferred to the mass transit account between 2011 and 2012 as states use some highway money for transit projects, as they are allowed.

Under those baseline assumptions, outlays would exceed revenues and interest credited to the highway account by about $5 billion in 2011 and by almost $10 billion in 2012. As a result, the highway account would be unable to meet its obligations sometime toward the end of fiscal year 2012 or early in fiscal year 2013, CBO estimates.[4] In all, outlays would exceed revenues and interest credited to the highway account by about $115 billion (or 31 percent) between 2011 and 2021.[5] If obligation limitations were held constant at 2011 amounts rather than increasing with inflation, that gap would be $85 billion (or 19 percent).

The situation for the Highway Trust Fund's mass transit account is similar. Under CBO's baseline projections and including transfers from the highway account, the obligation limitation for mass transit would grow from $9.3 billion in 2010 to $9.4 billion in 2012. Outlays would exceed revenues and interest credited to the mass transit account by about $2.5 billion in 2011 and by about $3.2 billion in 2012. The mass transit account would be able to meet obligations in a timely manner through 2012 but would be unable to meet some such obligations during 2013. Subsequently, projected spending from the transit account would exceed receipts by $4 billion to $5 billion a year, CBO projects.

Thus, future obligations for spending on transportation programs funded by the Highway Trust Fund will need to be significantly lower than in 2011, revenues available to the trust fund will need to be significantly higher, or both. If the Congress chose solely to cut spending, those cuts would need to decrease spending by about one-third. If the Congress chose to boost revenues, it could do so by increasing taxes that are dedicated to the Highway Trust Fund or by making transfers from the Treasury's general fund.

(Billions of 2010 dollars)

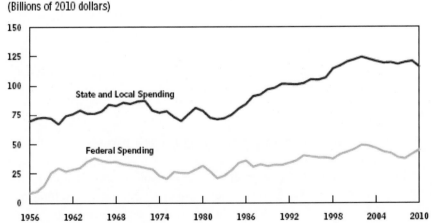

Source: Congressional Budget Office based on information from the Census Bureau and the Bureau of Economic Analysis.
Note: State and local spending from 2008 through 2010 were estimated by updating prior-year spending for changes in the value of state and local highways.

Figure 2. Spending for Highways, by Level of Government.

HOW MUCH SHOULD THE FEDERAL GOVERNMENT SPEND ON HIGHWAYS?

Almost all spending on highway infrastructure in the United States comes from public funds. The private sector participates in building, operating, and maintaining highways, but the federal government and state and local governments typically determine which projects to undertake and how much to spend on them. Despite several prominent examples of private financing for highways, private spending constitutes just a small share of the total. Spending by federal, state, and local governments has increased over the past half-century (see Figure 2). In 2010, the federal government spent $45 billion and state and local governments spent $116 billion on highways.

Determining whether the federal government—rather than state or local governments—should fund infrastructure projects depends, at least in part, on whether a project will benefit the nation as a whole more than it will a particular state or locality. Economic efficiency could be improved if the federal government limited its support to projects (such as the Interstate highways) that offer significant multistate benefits, leaving state and local governments to fund projects with more localized benefits. If the people who benefit from a project bear its costs, the likelihood is diminished that too large a project (or too many projects) will be undertaken or that too many infra-structure services will be consumed relative to the resources needed to provide them. In the past, the Congress also has considered other factors, including equity among the states and between urban and rural areas, in choosing which projects to fund.

Economic Returns on Public Spending for Highways

Highway spending has contributed to the nation's economic growth and prosperity and can continue to do so, depending on how and where funds are spent. Specifically, public investment in infrastructure can increase economic output by raising the stock of capital in the economy, thereby increasing the productivity of labor. Increasing transportation infrastructure would, in general, make it easier to move materials and workers to production facilities, supply finished goods to consumers, and transport service providers and customers to places of business. Consequently, workers would produce and deliver more in a given time and at a given cost. A more productive national economy would result in more goods and services and more resources for further investment and continued growth.

Over the past three decades, economists have produced a wide range of estimates of the benefits of investing in infrastructure.[6] A review of the literature indicates that the returns on investment in public capital in the United States are positive, although they are lower than some early estimates suggested. The literature also suggests that the returns on the initial phase of a system of public investments can be large but that the economic payoff declines as the system expands. In particular, economic gains from investing in highways appear to have been greatest during the initial construction of the Interstate Highway System and to have fallen off since then. According to one study of data spanning the period from 1953 to 1987, that initial construction made vehicle-intensive industries in particular more productive, but capital spending after the system was essentially completed in 1973 appeared not to have affected productivity in those industries.[7] Another study, which focused on the period after 1973, showed that even into the 1990s, the costs of logistics fell in vehicle-intensive industries because of highway improvements, although not as much as they had during the 1970s.[8] One 2006 report stated that every dollar of capital or maintenance spending for highways in 1996 reduced annual congestion costs to drivers by $0.11 that year.[9]

Total benefits over time would be greater, but whether they would be enough to justify the costs would depend on what else would be forgone to pay for more highway investment and the rate at which new or improved highways deteriorate.

Options for Federal Spending

The Congress faces difficult decisions about how much to spend on highways. The options include the following:

- Spend only what is collected from highway users through the gasoline and other taxes that are credited to the Highway Trust Fund;
- Maintain current capital spending, adjusted for inflation;
- Spend enough to maintain the highway system's current performance; or Fund projects whose expected benefits exceed costs by a particular amount.

Those options could be coupled with policies to manage use of highways by imposing congestion pricing during periods of peak demand.

Spend Revenues Credited to the Highway Trust Fund

The highway account of the trust fund received $30 billion in 2010 (see Figure 3). CBO projects that if current highway taxes are extended beyond their 2011 expiration date, revenues and interest credited to the Highway Trust Fund will rise at an average annual rate of a little more than 1 percent per year over the coming decade. That growth rate is slower than the expected growth in nominal gross domestic product, which CBO anticipates will increase by about 4 percent annually over the next 10 years—in part because fuel tax revenues depend on how much fuel is consumed and because fuel efficiency is expected to increase. Revenues for the highway account are projected to average $34 billion annually over the 2011–2021 period.

Maintain Current Capital Spending, Adjusted for Inflation

Total federal spending on highway infrastructure for 2010 amounted to $45 billion. Historically, federal spending for highway infrastructure has been predominantly for capital spending. Of that $45 billion, $43 billion was spent on capital projects, and $2 billion was spent on operations and maintenance. Real spending (that is, spending adjusted for inflation, in this case because of the rising costs of highway construction) by the federal government for highway construction has increased, on balance, over the past 30 years (see Figure 4). However, real spending declined in the middle of the 2000s, when the cost of materials increased sharply because of higher demand, attributable in part to a boom in residential and commercial construction in the United States and in part to increased demand from countries such as China.

Target Spending to Maintain Performance of Highways

Spending could instead be targeted to achieve specific goals for highway system performance, such as maintaining average delays or pavement quality. According to the FHWA, if current spending for highway capital was maintained over the coming decades, even adjusted for inflation, the performance and quality of the highway system would decline. On the basis of the FHWA's most recent projections (using 2006 data), CBO estimates that maintaining the current performance of the highway system would require $127 billion per year in combined capital spending by federal, state, and local governments.[10]

Historically, federal capital spending has constituted about 45 percent of all such spending. If the FHWA's assessment is accurate, and if the federal government funded a share of that total in proportion to its historical average, then the federal portion would be about $57 billion per year.

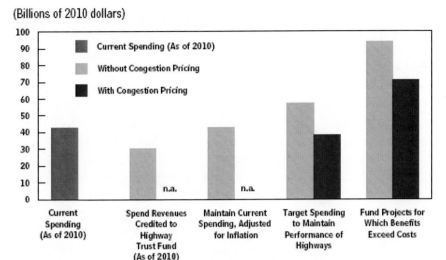

Source: Congressional Budget Office based on Department of Transportation, Federal
Highway Administration and Federal Transit Administration, 2008 Status of the
Nation's Highways, Bridges, and Transit: Conditions and Performance, Chapter 8.
Notes: Current spending is for capital projects and excludes $2 billion spent by the
federal government for operations and maintenance.
n.a. = not applicable.

Figure 3. Selected Options for Annual Federal Capital Spending for Highways, With
and Without Congestion Pricing.

That amount exceeds what the federal government actually spent in 2010
by $14 billion, or about one-third. State and local governments also would
need to increase their spending significantly to meet that target.

Fund Projects for Which Benefits Exceed Costs

By the FHWA's estimates, the amount of public spending that could be
justified for projects whose benefits outweigh their costs would be $209
billion per year. If the federal government maintained its historical share of
funding, federal annual capital spending for highways would need to be about
$94 billion, an increase of about $51 billion from the $43 billion spent in
2010; that increase would represent more than a doubling of federal spending.

Selecting projects carefully can increase the highway system's
contribution to the performance of the economy. Even within a group of
projects for which the benefits exceed the costs, some projects will offer
greater returns than others. Systematically ranking and funding projects to
identify those with the highest net benefits, and then undertaking those

projects, could yield a large share of total possible benefits at a lower overall cost. For example, if benefits had to exceed costs by some stated amount (such as 20 percent or 50 percent), those estimates of future spending would be lower. According to the FHWA's analysis, $188 billion per year would pay for all projects whose benefits outweighed their costs by at least 20 percent; and $165 billion would pay for projects whose benefits exceeded costs by at least 50 percent. In either scenario, travel delays and user costs would be less than they are currently, and pavement quality would be expected to improve.

The size of returns on investments in infrastructure depends on the investments undertaken and the type and amount of infrastructure already in place. For example, the FHWA groups capital spending into three categories, one each for expanding, enhancing, or rehabilitating highways. According to the FHWA's analysis of future needs, spending for Interstate highways should shift over time, going more toward expansion and less toward rehabilitation if the goal is to sustain the system's performance.[11]

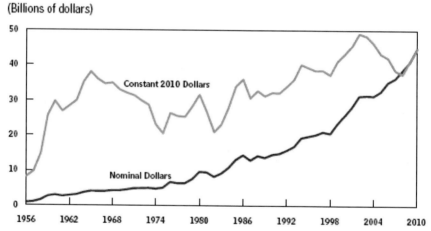

Source: Congressional Budget Office based on information from the Department of Commerce, Bureau of Economic Analysis.

Figure 4. Total Federal Spending for Highways, in Constant and Nominal Dollars.

Use Congestion Pricing

If highway users were charged fees that reflected the costs of driving when traffic was especially heavy, the existing infrastructure would be used more efficiently and the demand for future spending would be lower. Specifically, congestion pricing would result in fewer trips whose value to the driver was less than the costs of additional congestion imposed on other drivers. To the extent that some drivers would avoid paying a fee by choosing not to drive during peak hours, congestion would be reduced; the eventual outcome would be less need for spending on highways.[12]

According to the FHWA's estimates, widespread use of congestion pricing would reduce by nearly one-third the amount of capital investment needed to sustain the operational performance and condition of the highway system—from $127 billion per year to about $85 billion per year. The federal share, at the historical average of 45 percent, would be $38 billion—a little less than federal highway spending in 2010. Congestion pricing could reduce spending by about one-quarter, from $209 billion to $158 billion, for the set of projects for which benefits exceed costs. On the basis of historical averages, the federal share of that figure would be $71 billion.

HOW SHOULD THE FEDERAL GOVERNMENT DIRECT THE USE OF HIGHWAY FUNDS?

A second major issue facing the Congress is how best to direct federal spending for highways. From the point of view of economic efficiency, which level of government directs the use of highway funds should depend on who will benefit from the projects and who will bear the costs. The level of government with the incentives and information to weigh all of the costs and benefits is best positioned to make efficient decisions about highway investment.

If guided by that general principle, the federal government would select highway projects of national importance that provide broad geographic benefits, whereas state and local governments would be better situated to select highway projects if the benefits accrue primarily in their jurisdictions and their taxpayers would fund the projects. For projects that involve a mix of federal, state, and local benefits, efficiency is enhanced when decisionmaking can be coordinated among federal, state, and local governments and the costs can be shared. In contrast, transfers from the federal government may cause state and local governments to undertake some projects for which the costs exceed the benefits simply because federal money is available to be spent.

Some mechanisms that have been proposed would change the way the federal government directs a portion of spending for infrastructure, including highways, by placing decisions about which projects to fund in the hands of a federal infrastructure bank that selects projects on the basis of cost–benefit analysis rather than according to the geographic distribution of funds among the states. Concerns about project selection also have motivated federal and state initiatives to encourage private entities to finance highways.

Federal funds to support highway projects currently are provided in three different forms: grants to states; loan guarantees and other forms of credit assistance to states and localities; and tax preferences for debt issued by state and local governments for their own projects or for those undertaken by private entities on behalf of the public sector. In addition, partnerships between state and local governments and private entities sometimes use federal funds to support highway projects.

Federal Grants to States

About four-fifths of the funding appropriated to DOT for highways under SAFETEA-LU from 2005 to 2009 was distributed according to formulas. Those formulas allocated spending to states through various programs for constructing, improving, and maintaining highways and bridges; enhancing safety; reducing pollution; planning; and promoting alternative forms of transportation.[13] The formulas apply criteria that typically are related to the use and extent of state roadways (such as each state's share of highway lane-miles, vehicle-miles traveled, or fuel use) to determine a state's share of funds. An additional formula program, the Equity Bonus program, guarantees that each state's share is at least a specified percentage of that state's contributions to the highway account of the Highway Trust Fund. Once the Congress determines the formulas and the grants have been allocated, the states select the projects.

In most cases, the law requires that state and local governments match some portion—generally 20 percent—of federal highway funds.[14] If capital spending is anticipated to provide predominantly local benefits, however, the federal government could place more of the responsibility of paying for highway infrastructure with state and local governments by increasing the required matching rate. Evidence suggests that if federal spending decreases, state spending will increase somewhat. Confirming earlier analyses, the Government Accountability Office has reported that states reduced their own funding to offset roughly half of the increase in the federal highway grants that occurred during the 1990s.[15] Effectively, although an 80 percent federal contribution might be required to induce state and local spending on some projects that generate primarily national benefits, a smaller federal contribution might have been sufficient to foster state and local spending on most projects.

Raising the state and local matching rate above 20 percent would reduce the ability of those governments to substitute federal grants for their own funding and thereby divert to other uses some funds they otherwise would have spent on highways.

Moreover, formula grants are not closely linked to the performance of the transportation system. Although the current formulaic approaches to dividing federal resources for highways among the states may address notions of equity, the formulas do not necessarily promote the most economically advantageous projects. For example, the economic benefits of highway spending may be greater in areas with more traffic congestion or in areas of greater anticipated population growth and economic activity, but the current approach may direct federal resources to other areas. Similarly, costs to construct and improve highways could depend more on population density and geographic features than on other factors that are more important in the formulas, such as the size of a state's highway system and its recent volume of highway use.[16]

The remaining one-fifth of highway funding provided by SAFETEA-LU was allocated through mechanisms other than formulas to special-purpose programs and specific projects. The funds were divided among states on the basis of criteria specified in law or at the discretion of the Secretary of Transportation.

About half of that amount was directed by the Congress to individual projects, such as building a specific bridge or widening a particular stretch of road.

The Congress may specify particular projects for reasons it deems appropriate—equity, efficiency, or some other consideration— but to the extent that the selection of those projects gives little weight to efficiency, the federal government could promote effceincy by encouraging the funding of high-value projects through more systematic analyses of costs and benefits.

On occasion, highway funding has been distributed competitively to states and localities that apply for DOT funding. ARRA authorized $1.5 billion for the Transportation Investment Generating Economic Recovery program (known as TIGER), which provided grants that would fund up to 100 percent of the cost of various highway, bridge, transit, rail, and port projects. DOT chose state and local recipients on the basis of the results of cost–benefit analyses, among other criteria, and recipients had to demonstrate a significant benefit from the project for the nation, a region, or a metropolitan area.

Federal Loans and Loan Guarantees

The federal government also directs resources to state and local governments by providing and guaranteeing loans for infrastructure. Such credit assistance reduces state and local governments' costs because it allows borrowing at interest rates that are lower than otherwise might be available. Specifically, in providing loans and loan guarantees, the federal government assumes the risk that would be borne by a lender and paid for by a borrower in the form of higher interest rates.

The cost to the federal government of providing loans and loan guarantees largely depends on the cost of each loan and the number of loans made:

- The cost of each loan or loan guarantee depends on the creditworthiness of the projects financed by the loan and the structure of the loan. Creditworthiness depends on the borrower's likelihood of defaulting on the loan and on the lender's prospects for recovering the amounts owed if a default occurs. The loan's cost also depends on the structure of the loan, including the loan's period of repayment; the effective interest rate, including fees; whether the debt is subordinate to other debt (meaning that it is repaid only after other debts are repaid in the event of default); and whether the borrower can choose to defer payments to the federal government.

- The number of loans and loan guarantees made depends on demand and on limits on the amount of loans or loan guarantees that the government is authorized to make. Demand for loans and loan guarantees depends on the size of the subsidies provided and on how those subsidies compare with subsidies offered through the tax code and by other federal programs for financing infrastructure. Demand also is limited by the total value of loans that the federal government is authorized to make or guarantee. In some cases, appropriation acts specify a maximum amount of loans or guarantees. For most credit programs, however, the budget authority appropriated for the subsidy cost ultimately limits the number of loans issued or guaranteed.

The Federal Credit Reform Act of 1990 (FCRA) requires the subsidy costs of loans and loan guarantees to be calculated on an accrual basis—unlike most items in the federal budget, which are calculated on a cash basis—and those subsidy costs must be recorded in the budget when loans are disbursed and loan guarantees are committed to. As a result, the lifetime cost of a credit commitment is recognized in the year in which the loan or loan guarantee is made. The budgetary impact of most federal credit programs is calculated by that method.

The lifetime cost of a direct loan or loan guarantee is calculated as the net present value of expected cash flows over the life of the loan or loan guarantee (including any fees paid by the borrower to the government).[17] Under FCRA, net present value is estimated by discounting cash flows back to the time a loan is disbursed or commitment of a loan guarantee is made using the interest rates on Treasury securities of comparable maturity. (For example, cash flows that will occur one year after disbursement are discounted using the rate on one-year Treasury securities; flows that will occur five years out are discounted using the five-year rate; and so on.)

The budgetary cost of a credit program tends to be lower than the budgetary cost of an economically equivalent grant or benefit payment because FCRA accounting does not provide a comprehensive measure of the economic cost of credit assistance. Through its use of Treasury rates for discounting, FCRA implicitly treats market risk—a type of risk that investors require compensation to bear—as having no cost to the government. Specifically, FCRA's procedures incorporate the expected cost of defaults on government loans or loan guarantees but not the cost of uncertainty about the magnitude of those defaults. Investors require compensation (a "market risk premium") to bear certain types of risk. The market risk premium on a risky loan or guarantee compensates investors for the increased likelihood of sustaining a loss when the overall economy is weak and resources are scarce; that likelihood is reflected in higher expected returns and lower prices for assets that carry more market risk. Taxpayers bear the investment risk for federal credit obligations. When a borrower defaults on a loan, the loss ultimately must be covered by higher taxes or by reduced spending on other programs. By omitting the cost of market risk and thereby understating the economic cost of federal credit obligations, FCRA accounting may lead policymakers to favor credit assistance over other forms of aid that have a similar economic cost.[18]

An important aspect of the budgetary treatment of federal credit programs is that agencies must receive an appropriation equal to the estimated subsidy cost before they can make or guarantee a loan. In the case of direct loans, FCRA specifies that loan repayments are unavailable for future spending; those repayments are already accounted for in the estimated net present value of the loan, so they are not available to "revolve" into new loans. Such a revolving fund is the model on which many state infrastructure banks are based. However, for the federal government, those repayments represent part of the financing for the original loans and are implicit in the subsidy calculation. Allowing loan repayments to be used for new loans—without any additional appropriation to cover the subsidy costs of the new loans—would raise the effective subsidy cost on the original loans to 100 percent (the same as for grants).

Because the federal budget records the lifetime cost of loans and loan guarantees rather than the initial amount of lending, loans and loan guarantees with a given budgetary cost lead to more money flowing initially to projects than if that same budgetary cost was incurred through grants or other direct payments to the states. As a result, credit assistance initially provides greater leverage for federal funds than grants and other direct payments do. Unlike grants and other direct payments, however, funds borrowed under credit assistance programs ultimately must be repaid by state and local governments or by users of the projects that are financed by the credit.

A program created by the Transportation Infrastructure Finance and Innovation Act of 1992 (TIFIA) provides credit assistance for highways and other types of surface transportation infrastructure. Some recent proposals would create a federal infrastructure bank to offer similar assistance under a different organizational structure.[19] Whether federal credit assistance is provided through a federal program or a special entity, however, it involves similar budgetary costs to the federal government. Therefore, differences between the existing TIFIA program and an infrastructure bank would be primarily operational, concerning the scope of infrastructure to fund, the kinds of credit assistance to provide, the selection process for projects, the amount of leverage to provide for federal funds, and the amount of private-sector participation to encourage or require.

Transportation Infrastructure Finance and Innovation Act

The TIFIA program offers federal loans to qualifying state and local projects for up to 35 years at the interest rate on a Treasury security of similar maturity. (For example, 4.26 percent was the rate for a 30-year Treasury bond as of May 5, 2011.) It also provides loan guarantees and lines of credit. TIFIA assistance can be used for up to one-third of a project's costs.

DOT administers the TIFIA program and selects projects on the basis of criteria, established by statute, that include an analysis of a project's benefits and costs and whether it has national or regional significance. Loans made by the federal government at Treasury rates for risky projects represent taxpayer-financed subsidies, and riskier projects involve larger subsidies. TIFIA loans are restricted to projects that are considered relatively safe—as evidenced by a high rating from a credit-rating agency—to keep the subsidy rate relatively low. (Subsidy rates average around 10 percent.) As access to credit became more restricted during the recent financial crisis, demand for TIFIA assistance outpaced availability, and project selection became competitive.

Several features of the TIFIA program attract private finance. The program subsidizes credit assistance, and TIFIA loans encourage private-sector participation by having lower priority for repayment than private debt in the event of a default.[20] TIFIA's loan terms also allow private managers to defer repayment for up to five years after a project's completion—a valuable benefit, for example, if there is uncertainty about how much toll revenue a highway project will generate.

From fiscal year 2005 through fiscal year 2010, the TIFIA program provided about $5 billion in loans for highways, transit, and intermodal projects, supporting $18 billion worth of projects. As authorized by SAFETEA-LU and its extensions, TIFIA received about $732 million of budget authority over that period.

Proposals for a Federal Infrastructure Bank

In recent years, the Congress has considered several proposals for establishing a federal bank to fund infrastructure projects through loans and grants. The President's budget requests have suggested creating a similar entity. In principle, an infrastructure bank could use any of several methods to finance projects, including providing federal loans, lines of credit, and guarantees for private loans. Moreover, some proposals suggest mechanisms for disbursing grants to fund projects that would not create enough revenue to repay a loan.

An infrastructure bank could focus on financing transportation infrastructure, or it could define infrastructure more broadly to include sewers, wastewater treatment facilities, drinking water supply facilities, broadband Internet access, or even schools. A federal infrastructure bank could be located within an existing federal agency, such as DOT or the Treasury, or it could be created as a separate entity. Most proposals would have such a bank select projects on merit, considering, for example, their likely impact on the national or regional economy.

Some financial and transportation analysts contend that making funds available through an infrastructure bank would encourage state and local governments to work together across jurisdictional lines and transportation modes to plan and complete comprehensive projects. For example, an infrastructure bank could participate in developing projects that involve more than one mode of transportation—although the Congress could encourage this otherwise through language authorizing more funding for mass transit or other projects involving more than one mode of transportation. As another example, an infrastructure bank could fund cross-jurisdictional projects by helping different government entities gain coordinated access to credit markets.

Other analysts point to the potential capacity of an infrastructure bank to use cost– benefit analysis effectively in project selection. The capacity of state and local governments to complete such analyses varies significantly, and proponents believe that a bank could help bolster that capacity nationwide, thus leading to better selection of projects overall.

In addition, some financial and transportation analysts suggest that an infrastructure bank could encourage more private funding of infrastructure projects by using funds more efficiently than occurs under the current system of distributing formula grants. By providing federal funds that reduce the amount of private investment a project requires, for example, an infrastructure bank could allow projects that rely on tolls or other funding mechanisms to offer returns sufficient to attract private-sector participation. As a result, private-sector entities, in conjunction with state and local governments, could choose to fund projects that, in the absence of federal financial assistance, would not be built.

Regardless of how it was constituted, however, an infrastructure bank would be unlikely to supplant the established methods of distributing most federal infrastructure funds. One limitation is that few surface transportation projects are good candidates for bank funding because they mostly do not involve toll collections or other mechanisms for charging users directly to repay construction loans. Furthermore, about three-quarters of current federal funds spent on surface transportation are used to maintain existing infrastructure. Those projects are not good candidates for funding from an infrastructure bank because, in general, they would not generate revenue that could be used to repay loans.

Tax Preferences

The federal government provides several types of tax preferences for infrastructure financing. Tax-exempt bonds use the well-established tax preference of paying interest that is not subject to federal income tax. Such bonds can be issued to finance either the functions of state and local governments or certain projects undertaken by the private sector. A second, more recent type of tax preference for infrastructure financing is used by tax credit bonds. Such bonds come in two basic forms: those that provide a tax credit to the bondholder in lieu of interest and those that provide a tax credit to the bond issuer, payable by the Secretary of the Treasury. Tax-exempt and tax credit bonds alike transfer some of the cost of borrowing from state and local governments and the private sector to the federal government in the form of forgone federal tax revenues.

In contrast to grants and credit assistance, tax preferences are outside the annual appropriation process, so the federal government may exercise less oversight over their allocation. Also, because forgone revenues do not appear directly in the federal budget, the use of tax preferences can mask the full scope of the government's financial activities. Moreover, some tax preferences are an inefficient way to deliver a federal financial subsidy to state and local governments. With a tax exemption for interest income, for example, state and local borrowing costs are reduced by significantly less than the federal revenues that are forgone, and the remainder of that tax expenditure accrues to bond buyers in the highest income tax brackets. Modifying federal tax preferences for infrastructure financing by increasing the use of tax credit payments made directly to borrowers can improve both budgetary practice and economic efficiency.[21]

Tax-Exempt Bonds

Federal tax exemptions for interest income from government bonds (and qualified private activity bonds—bonds issued by a government on behalf of a private entity—under certain circumstances) enable issuers of such debt to sell bonds that pay lower rates of interest than do taxable bonds with the same maturity, risk, and so on. Because purchasers of tax-exempt bonds demand a return that is at least as high as the after-tax yield they could obtain from comparable taxable bonds, the amount by which the return from tax-exempt bonds is lower than the yield on comparable taxable bonds depends on the income tax rate of the marginal (or market-clearing) buyer of tax-exempt bonds.[22]

The amount of subsidy that state and local borrowers receive by issuing tax-exempt bonds is largely determined indirectly by the federal tax code. Data on tax-exempt and taxable bond transactions allow estimation of the marginal tax rate faced by the market-clearing buyer of tax-exempt bonds and, thus, the amount that states and localities save in financing costs by issuing such bonds. In 2007, the average yield on (taxable) high-grade corporate bonds was 5.6

percent, and the average yield on tax-exempt municipal bonds of similar creditworthiness was 4.4 percent—a difference of 1.2 percentage points, or approximately 21 percent of the taxable return. That 21 percent also represents the marginal tax rate at which an investor would be indifferent between purchasing a taxable bond yielding 5.6 percent and a tax-exempt bond yielding 4.4 percent. Thus, the market-clearing investor in 2007 paid income tax at a rate of 21 percent—which is also the average implicit income tax rate observed for such buyers of tax-exempt bonds during the two decades just before that, according to the staff of the Joint Committee on Taxation.[23] Investors' appetite for risk, the desired time-horizon of their investments, and other bond-specific features can also influence the demand for taxable and tax-exempt debt. The implicit tax rate of the marginal buyer of tax-exempt bonds fell to an average of about 15 percent per year from 2008 to 2010 because turbulence in financial markets led investors to favor less risky debt—such as U.S. Treasury securities—which reduced the yield on those securities relative to tax-exempt debt.[24]

However, the loss in federal revenues results from both the market-clearing investor and investors in higher income tax brackets. Several analysts suggest that about 80 percent of the tax expenditure from tax-exempt bonds translates into lower borrowing costs for states and localities, with the remaining 20 percent taking the form of a federal transfer to bondholders in higher tax brackets.[25] If 20 percent of the federal revenue loss from tax-exempt bonds accrued to that group without lowering borrowing costs, and if the outstanding stock of tax-exempt debt for infrastructure during the 2010–2014 period instead took the form of tax credit bonds designed to deliver the same amount of interest subsidy per year, the federal government would save more than $32 billion (20 percent of an estimated $162 billion in tax expenditure).[26] Moreover, a direct appropriation of funds would purchase more infrastructure per dollar of impact on the federal budget.

Tax Credit Bonds

Starting in the late 1990s, the Congress turned to tax credit bonds as a way to finance public expenditures. In their early form, tax credit bonds allow bondholders to receive a credit against federal income tax liability instead of— or in addition to—the cash interest typically paid on the bonds. The amount of tax credit equals the credit rate, which is set by the Secretary of the Treasury, multiplied by the face amount of the holder's bond. Because bondholders pay taxes on the amount of credit they claim, tax credit bonds do not, in contrast to tax-exempt debt, provide a revenue transfer to investors in high marginal tax brackets. As a result, the revenues forgone by the federal government through tax credit bonds reduce state and local borrowing costs dollar for dollar. Tax credit bonds also allow the amount of federal subsidy to be determined independent of other federal policy decisions (such as marginal income tax rates). Thus, tax credit bonds offer the promise of increasing the efficiency and equity with which federal resources are allocated to support infrastructure and other investments. ARRA authorized Build America Bonds, a new type of tax credit bond that was sold only in 2009 and 2010. State and local governments were authorized to issue Build America Bonds either as traditional tax credit bonds or, if certain conditions were met, as direct-pay tax credit bonds (known as qualified Build America Bonds). In contrast to earlier tax credit bonds, Build America Bonds have an interest rate (or coupon) that is set by the issuer rather than by the Secretary of the Treasury. In the direct-pay scenario, a credit equal to 35 percent of each interest payment could be claimed by the issuer in lieu of a tax credit going to the bondholder. Because state and local governments issuing direct-pay Build America Bonds are not liable for taxes on that credit, they pay less interest than they would for Build America Bonds that provide the credit to the bondholder. As a result, the direct-pay version of Build America Bonds proved to be the one used by issuers. Sales of those bonds financed $38 billion in transportation spending in 2009 and 2010.[27]

Direct-pay tax credit bonds offer several advantages over other types of tax-preferred bonds. Making a payment directly to state and local governments to compensate them for the interest they pay on a direct-pay tax credit bond is a more cost-effective way to provide a federal financing subsidy than offering a tax exemption on interest income. And unlike other tax preferences, interest subsidies on direct-pay bonds appear as outlays in the federal budget, making the cost of that financial subsidy more transparent and, in principle, enabling comparison with other federal outlays for the same purposes. Also, because the yields provided to holders of direct-pay tax credit bonds are similar to the yields of other taxable securities, direct-pay tax credit bonds are more attractive to tax-exempt entities than other tax credit bonds and thereby potentially increase the pool of funds available to state and local governments to finance their investments in infrastructure and other activities.

Public–Private Partnerships

Public and private financing are distinguished by the entity that issues debt or raises equity to provide the funds for a project. In the traditional approach to building highways, a state or local government uses its own tax receipts, federal grants, public bond issues, and sometimes toll revenues to cover the costs of construction. In public– private partnerships that include private financing, the private partner enters into contracts with a state or local government to build and finance a highway in exchange for future payments from the public sector or the right to collect toll revenues. To finance construction, the private entity usually raises equity or borrows in the private capital market. It does so with the expectation that some combination of future toll revenues and payments from state and local governments will cover the project's costs, which include debt payments and a market return to equity holders.

Although private sources can provide additional financing for infrastructure, that financing needs to earn a return over time—and the ultimate sources of payment for the return on private financing are the same as the sources of public financing, namely taxes or user fees. Therefore, private financing does not provide truly new resources for infrastructure investment.

Still, an argument is sometimes made that public–private partnerships can accelerate the availability of funds for infrastructure investment by tapping private capital markets in ways that governments cannot or will not. That contention holds only in the context of the legal constraints that states and localities face and in the context of their budgetary practices. For example, many states and localities have statutory or constitutional limits on borrowing, and budgetary practices used to assess borrowing generally include standard debt instruments but may not include other types of future obligations, such as those made through public–private partnerships. Although some limits are informal or easily bypassed, many limits cannot be raised without voter approval or a legislative supermajority. When limits cannot be raised, states may turn to private debt or equity to finance roads. Traditional financing is therefore restricted not only by constituent aversion to taxes, which provide the stream of revenues that make bond issuance possible, but also by statutory or constitutional limits on borrowing.

Several privately financed highway projects that relied on toll revenues have struggled financially, beset by inaccurate revenue projections and encumbered with high debt service payments. As a result, subsequent projects that are still under construction have been put together differently, reducing the private partner's exposure to the uncertainty of demand for driving on the highway and keeping down debt service payments, which have amounted to the largest continuing cost for past projects with private financing. States more commonly offer private partners state revenues— so-called availability payments—instead of, or in addition to, tolls; in doing so, they assume a part of the risk that tolls will fall short of expectations. Project debt service payments are being reduced by increasing the amount of public financing through state and federal programs, such as the use of private activity bonds and the federal TIFIA program. Those changes have brought public–private partnerships with private financing more in line with the traditional methods of financing highway construction.

HOW SHOULD THE FEDERAL GOVERNMENT RAISE FUNDS FOR HIGHWAYS?

About 10 percent of all funding for highways, by all levels of government, comes from issuing bonds (see Figure 5).

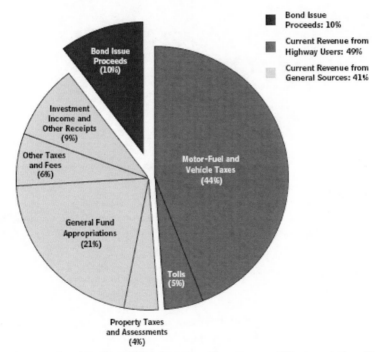

Source: Congressional Budget Office based on Department of Transportation, Federal Highway Administration, Highway Statistics 2008 (December 2009), Table HF-10.

Figure 5. Sources of Funding for Highways, All Levels of Government, 2008.

The remaining 90 percent comes from the combination of current revenue collected from highway users and, to a slightly lesser extent, current revenue collected from general sources. Of course, all of the costs of building and maintaining highways are ultimately borne by users and taxpayers, regardless of whether governments or private entities pay for highways now or borrow funds and repay them over time. About three-quarters of the amount paid for debt service on bonds comes from taxes and tolls imposed on highway users; the balance comes from general revenues and interest income (see Figure 6).

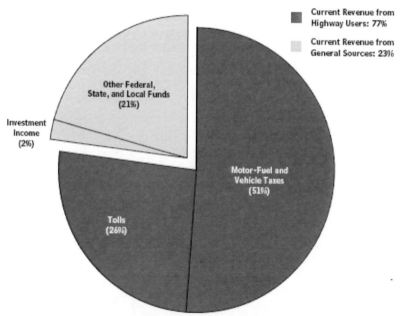

Source: Congressional Budget Office based on Department of Transportation, Federal
    Highway Administration, Highway Statistics 2008 (December 2009), Table SB-3.
Note: Excludes proceeds from sales of other bonds.

Figure 6. Sources of Funding for Paying Debt Service on Bond Issues, All Levels of Government, 2008.

Approaches to funding highways can be evaluated in terms of equity and economic efficiency. Equity is a subjective attribute that can be assessed in several ways. Observers of highway funding often gauge equity by considering the share of funding that is obtained from taxes paid by highway users (rather than from general taxpayer funds), from people in households that fall into various income categories, or from people in rural versus urban households.

The economic efficiency of a funding approach depends partly on its effects on users' travel behavior and partly on what it costs to implement. Charging users for the costs that their travel imposes on society would create incentives for people to limit highway use to trips for which the benefits exceed the costs, thus reducing or eliminating overuse of highways and helping identify the economic value of investments in highways. However, the costs of collecting and enforcing such user charges also influence the efficiency of that approach.

User Charges

Economic efficiency is promoted when highway users are charged according to the marginal (or incremental) costs of their use, including external costs that are imposed on society. A combination of a fuel tax and a mileage-based tax (a VMT tax) that accounts for the type and weight of a vehicle and the location and time of its use could provide incentives for reducing the full range of driving's social costs and could generate funds for federal spending on highways.

The external costs of highway use vary widely depending on the characteristics of a vehicle and where it is driven. Some external costs are associated directly with the use of motor fuel, such as the costs of local air pollution from trucks, climate change, and dependence on foreign oil. Those costs are estimated to average more than 30 cents per gallon for passenger vehicles and more than 70 cents per gallon for trucks (see Figure 7). Other external costs are related to the miles traveled by vehicles, such as the costs of road congestion, pavement damage, and accidents. Although the external costs imposed on society by trucks are greater than those imposed by passenger vehicles on a per-mile basis, the much higher volume of passenger vehicle travel means that those vehicles also contribute substantially to external costs from vehicle-miles traveled (see Figure 8).

Specifically, passenger vehicles account for more than 90 percent of vehicle-miles traveled, with passenger vehicles in urban areas alone accounting for more than 60 percent. Passenger vehicles' contribution to traffic congestion in urban areas imposes estimated costs of about 10 cents per mile, on average, constituting one of the largest sources of total external costs of motor vehicle use.

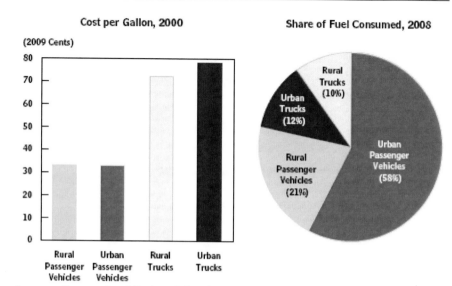

Cost per Gallon, 2000

Share of Fuel Consumed, 2008

Sources: Congressional Budget Office based on Ian W.H. Parry, "How Should Heavy-Duty Trucks Be Taxed?" Journal of Urban Economics, vol. 63, no. 2 (March 2008), p. 660; and Department of Transportation, Federal Highway Administration, Highway Statistics 2008 (December 2009), Table VM-1.

Notes: Passenger vehicles have two axles and four tires and include automobiles and light trucks (pickup trucks, minivans, and sport-utility vehicles). Fuel use shares exclude motorcycles and buses. Local air pollution costs are classified as mileage related for passenger vehicles and fuel related for trucks.

Figure 7. Estimated Fuel-Related Costs and Fuel Consumed in Various Years.

Estimates of pavement damage by trucks, the largest per-mile external cost of truck use, average roughly 15 cents and 40 cents per mile in rural and urban areas—making those vehicles another significant source of external costs, even though truck travel represents less than 10 percent of all miles traveled.

For different trucks, pavement damage costs vary widely, depending on the weight of the truck and the number of axles over which the weight is distributed. Accidents, noise, air pollution, and other fuel-related costs from passenger vehicles and trucks represent smaller shares of external costs.

Just as the external costs of highway use are related to fuel use and miles traveled, user charges can take the form of fuel taxes and mileage-based fees. Those charges differ in the administrative costs they entail, how efficiently they match the external costs that users impose, and in the extent to which they are borne by people in different income groups or different locations.

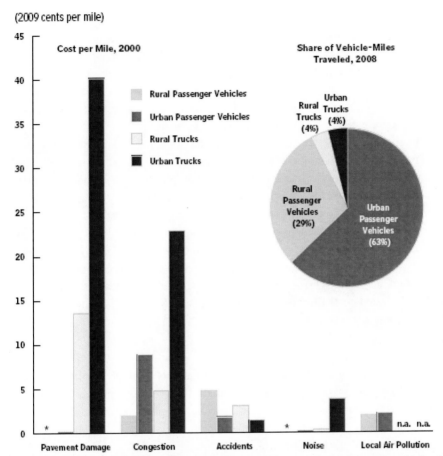

Sources: Congressional Budget Office based on Department of Transportation, Federal
   Highway Administration, 1997 Federal Highway Cost Allocation Study Final
   Report (1997), Tables V-22 (noise), V-23 (congestion), V-24 (accidents), and V-
   26 (pavement damage); Addendum to the 1997 Federal Highway Cost Allocation
   Study Final Report (May 2000), Table 13; and Highway Statistics 2008
   (December 2009), Table VM-1.
Notes: Passenger vehicles have two axles and four tires and include automobiles and
   light trucks (pickup trucks, minivans, and sport-utility vehicles). Mileage shares
   exclude motorcycles and buses. Local air pollution costs are classified as mileage
   related for passenger vehicles and fuel related for trucks.
* = less than 0.5 cents per mile; n.a. = not applicable.

Figure 8. Estimated Mileage-Related Costs and Vehicle-Miles Traveled in Various
Years.

Fuel Taxes

Viewed according to different conceptions of equity, fuel taxes offer a mix of positive and negative characteristics. They satisfy a "user-pays" criterion, but they also can impose a larger burden relative to income on people who live in low-income or rural households. Fuel taxes impose a burden even on households that do not own passenger vehicles by raising transportation costs, which are reflected in the prices of purchased goods.

Fuel taxes have two desirable characteristics for efficiency: They cost relatively little to implement (the government collects taxes from fuel distributors, and users pay the taxes when they purchase fuel), and they offer users some incentive to curtail fuel use, thus reducing some of the social costs of travel. At best, however, a fuel tax discourages some travel too much and other travel too little, because it does not reflect the large differences in cost for use of crowded roads compared with uncrowded roads or for travel by trucks that have similar fuel efficiency but cause different amounts of pavement damage. Moreover, for a given tax rate on fuels, the incentive to reduce mileage-related costs diminishes over time as more driving is done in vehicles that are more fuel efficient.

VMT Taxes

VMT taxes and fuel taxes have qualitatively similar implications for equity. Like fuel taxes, VMT charges satisfy the user-pays principle, but they impose larger burdens relative to income on people in low-income or rural households. To the extent that members of such households tend to drive vehicles that are less fuel efficient, such as pickup trucks or older automobiles, however, those highway users would pay a smaller share of VMT taxes than of fuel taxes.

VMT taxes would provide stronger incentives than fuel taxes could for efficient use of highways if VMT taxes were aligned with the costs imposed by users, because most of those costs are related to the number of miles driven. Appropriately aligned, VMT taxes could meet various goals, including paying for pavement damage, reducing congestion (and thus curtailing the need to spend money on highway expansion and highway maintenance), or fostering efficient use with regard to all social costs.

If VMT taxes were intended to maximize or even significantly improve the efficiency of highway use, they would need to vary greatly by vehicle type, by time and place of travel, or both. For example, because pavement damage increases sharply with vehicle weight but decreases with the number of axles on a vehicle, the portion of VMT taxes assessed to maintain pavement could be small or nonexistent for passenger vehicles but substantial for heavy-duty trucks, particularly those with high weight per axle. Similarly, every vehicle would be assessed more to travel on crowded urban roads during peak hours than in off-peak hours or to travel on less congested roads at any time. The rates charged for peak-hour travel would be set in keeping with specific local or regional conditions, including the duration and severity of daily congestion, rather than on the basis of national averages.

VMT taxes' effect on efficiency also would depend on how much it costs to put the taxes in place and to collect the money. Estimates of what it would cost to establish and operate a nationwide program are rough. One source of uncertainty is the cost to install metering equipment in the nation's cars and trucks. Having the devices installed as original equipment under a mandate to vehicle manufacturers would be relatively inexpensive but could lead to a long transition; requiring all vehicles to be retrofitted with devices could be faster but much more costly, and the equipment could be more susceptible to tampering than factory-installed equipment might be. Despite the various uncertainties and impediments, some transportation experts have identified VMT taxes as a preferred option.

The idea of imposing VMT taxes that vary by time and place has raised concerns about privacy because the process of assessing such taxes could give the government access to specific information about how individual vehicles are used. Various approaches have been suggested to allay those concerns, including restricting the amount of travel-related information that could be used for billing or restricting the kind of information conveyed to the government; making devices appealing to the public by allowing businesses to use them to provide other services, such as real-time traffic reports or electronic payment for parking; and allowing users to choose not to pay per-mile charges but to pay higher fuel taxes instead. (Under such proposals, the optional fuel taxes would be set at rates high enough to appeal only to users with the greatest privacy concerns.)

A system of VMT taxes need not apply to all vehicles on every road. Indeed, there are already less comprehensive systems of direct charges for road use: Toll roads, lanes, and bridges are common in the United States, and several states and foreign countries place weight-and-distance taxes on trucks. Expansion of existing systems could focus on highly congested roads or on entry points into congested areas; that targeted approach could cost less to implement if it required relatively simple in-vehicle equipment. Alternatively, the focus could be on specific vehicle types, such as trucks.

Although only 4 percent of the nation's fleet is made up of trucks (excluding light-duty trucks), they account for roughly 25 percent of all costs that highway users impose on others, including almost all of the costs associated with pavement damage.

General Revenues from Taxpayers

Two arguments can be made in support of funding highways with broad-based taxes, such as income taxes: First, the incremental costs of collection would be negligible, and second, large amounts could be raised through small changes in tax rates. The staff of the Joint Committee on Taxation has estimated that raising all tax rates on ordinary individual income by 1 percentage point would yield an average of $48 billion per year from 2012 to 2021—more than all of the current Highway Trust Fund taxes combined.[28] Moreover, funding highways through broad-based taxes meets at least one standard of equity: Such taxes do not impose a larger burden relative to income on rural or low-income users.

In other respects, however, the use of general revenues poses significant disadvantages. In particular, the approach gives users no incentive to reduce the mileage- or fuel-related costs of their highway use, and it does not satisfy the user-pays standard of equity. Moreover, even small increases in existing rates would hamper efficiency by exacerbating existing deviations from efficient prices, thus further distorting many individual decisions. The distorted decisions would include reductions in work and saving, shifting of income from taxable to nontaxable forms, and shifting of spending from ordinary to tax-deductible goods and services.

End Notes

[1]. See Congressional Budget Office, Alternative Approaches to Funding Highways (March 2011); Spending and Funding for Highways, Issue Brief (January 2011); and Public Spending on Transportation and Water Infrastructure (November 2010).

[2] An authorization act is a law under the jurisdiction of a committee other than the House or Senate Committee on Appropriations. Budget authority is the authority provided by law to incur financial obligations that will result in immediate or future outlays of federal government funds.

[3] An obligation limitation is a provision of a law or legislation that restricts or reduces the availability of budget authority that would have become available under another law (in this case, the authorizing law).

[4] Under current law, the Highway Trust Fund cannot incur negative balances. If the trust fund is unable to meet its obligations in a timely manner, spending could continue more slowly, to keep pace with tax collections. DOT has stated that, in the event of a shortfall, reimbursements to states would be rationed to maintain a positive balance.

[5] CBO's projections of spending from the trust fund are based on historical averages, but actual spending will differ from projections from year to year depending on such factors as the states' construction schedules and plans. Future revenues might differ from CBO's projections depending on changes in the price of oil, the economy, and the fuel efficiency of vehicles. Small deviations from the projections of spending and revenues, however, would not significantly affect the status of the Highway Trust Fund or the expected imbalance between obligations and resources.

[6] See Congressional Budget Office, Issues and Options in Infrastructure Investment (May 2008); and The Economic Effects of Federal Spending on Infrastructure and Other Investments (June 1998).

[7] See John Fernald, "Roads to Prosperity? Assessing the Link Between Public Capital and Prosperity," American Economic Review, vol. 89, no. 3 (June 1999), pp. 619–638.

[8] See Chad Shirley and Clifford Winston, "Firm Inventory Behavior and the Returns from Highway Infrastructure Investments," Journal of Urban Economics, vol. 55, no. 2 (May 2004), pp. 398–415.

[9] Congestion costs reflect both the amount of gasoline consumed and the value of the time that motorists lose to traffic delays. See Clifford M. Winston and Ashley Langer, "The Effect of Government Highway Spending on Road Users' Congestion Costs," Journal of Urban Economics, vol. 60, no. 3 (November 2006), pp. 463–483.

[10]. See Department of Transportation, Federal Highway Administration and Federal Transit Administration, 2008 Status of the Nation's Highways, Bridges, and Transit: Conditions and Performance, pp. ix, xii. The FHWA's report defines the system's performance in terms of average user costs, including the costs of travel time, operations, and accidents. The FHWA's estimate is similar to the $131 billion (in 2008 dollars) estimated by the Congressionally chartered National Surface Transportation Infrastructure Financing Commission for the average annual spending needed to maintain the current performance of the highway system. See National Surface Transportation Infrastructure Financing Commission, Paying Our Way: A New Framework for Transportation Finance (February 2009), p. 53. Unless otherwise noted, figures in the text that are based on the FHWA's spending estimates are expressed in 2010 dollars.

[11] Department of Transportation, 2008 Status of the Nation's Highways, Bridges, and Transit, Chapter 8.

[12] For a comprehensive discussion of the benefits and challenges of congestion pricing, including options for its design and implementation for highways, see Congressional Budget Office, Using Pricing to Reduce Traffic Congestion (March 2009).

[13] See Department of Transportation, Federal Highway Administration, Highway Statistics 2009 (December 2009), Table FA-4A, for a list of 2010 apportionment formulas. For descriptions of various programs see Department of Transportation, Federal Highway Administration, "Fact Sheets on Highway Programs," www.fhwa.dot.gov/safetealu/factsheets.htm.

[14] In general, the match is smaller for some projects on Interstate highways and for projects in states with high concentrations of tribal or federal land.

[15] See Government Accountability Office, Federal-Aid Highways: Trends, Effects on State Spending, and Options for Future Program Design, GAO-04-802 (August 2004), www.gao.gov/products/ GAO-04-802.

[16] For a discussion of the importance of performance metrics for transportation, see National Transportation Policy Project, *Performance Driven: A New Vision for U.S. Transportation Policy* (Washington, D.C.: Bipartisan Policy Center, June 2009), www.bipartisanpolicy. org/library/report/ performance-driven.

[17] Present value is a single number that expresses a flow of current and future payments in terms of an equivalent lump sum received today. Thus, a $100 million, 30-year loan disbursed in 2011 that is determined to have a subsidy cost of 10 percent would be recorded as $10 million in budget authority and $10 million in outlays on the budget that year. The cash flows repaid to the government over the next 30 years (principal and interest) would not be recorded on the budget (except for credit reestimates, which are adjustments made to the original subsidy rate).

[18] Moreover, subsidy rates computed under FCRA exclude federal administrative costs, even those that are essential for preserving the value of the government's claim to future repayments, such as loan servicing and collection costs; those costs are accounted for separately in the budget.

[19] Other government programs that provide credit assistance for infrastructure projects include the Environmental Protection Agency's grants for states' revolving loan funds for water projects and states' infrastructure banks, all of which are capitalized with federal funds and administered by states.

[20]. However, upon bankruptcy, insolvency, or liquidation of an asset backed by a TIFIA loan, that loan would have equal priority with private debt in its claim for repayment.

[21] For a more complete discussion of how federal tax preferences operate in financing investment in highways and other infrastructure, see Congressional Budget Office and Joint Committee on Taxation, *Subsidizing Infrastructure Investment with Tax-Preferred Bonds* (October 2009).

[22] Issuers of tax-exempt debt need to increase the interest rate they pay until the pool of bond purchasers is large enough to purchase all of the debt the issuers are bringing to market. The marginal buyer of tax-exempt bonds will typically demand a higher tax-exempt yield than someone in a higher income tax bracket does. Issuers raise the interest rate enough that the yield on tax-exempt bonds is competitive with the rate of return on taxable instruments (after taking taxes into account) to draw in bond buyers from lower income tax brackets. The market-clearing buyer thus determines the interest rate that issuers of tax-exempt bonds must pay—and, implicitly, the savings in financing costs that issuers enjoy relative to issuing taxable debt.

[23] See Joint Committee on Taxation, *Present Law and Issues Related to Infrastructure Finance*, JCX-83-08 (October 24, 2008), p. 28, www.house.gov/jct/x-83-08.pdf.

[24] CBO calculation based on Council of Economic Advisers, *Economic Report of the President* (February 2011), Table B-73, p. 276, www.gpoaccess.gov/eop/.

[25] See Dennis Zimmerman, *The Private Use of Tax-Exempt Bonds: Controlling Public Subsidy of Private Activity* (Washington, D.C.: Urban Institute Press, 1991), pp. 103–104; and James Poterba and Ramirez Verdugo, *Portfolio Substitution and the Revenue Cost of Exempting State and Local Government Interest Payments from Federal Income Tax*, Working Paper 14439 (Cambridge, Mass.: National Bureau of Economic Research, October 2008), www.nber.org/papers/w14439.

[26] In addition to being an inefficient means of providing a subsidy for debt financing, tax-exempt bonds also are regressive: The amount by which the benefits captured by an investor exceeds the issuer's cost savings increases with the investor's marginal tax rate. One study estimates that eliminating the tax exemption on state and local debt would reduce after-tax

income primarily for taxpayers in the highest income quintile—and particularly for individuals in the top 1 percent of the income distribution. See Leonard Burman, Eric Toder, and Christopher Geissler, *How Big Are Total Individual Income Tax Expenditures, and Who Benefits from Them?* Discussion Paper 31 (Washington, D.C.: Urban Institute, December 2008), p. 11, www.urban.org/publications/ 1001234.html.

[27] Section 301 of the Hiring Incentives to Restore Employment Act extended the direct-pay provision to other tax credit bonds: new clean renewable energy bonds, qualified energy conservation bonds, qualified zone academy bonds, and qualified school construction bonds (also authorized by ARRA).

[28] See Congressional Budget Office, *Reducing the Deficit: Spending and Revenue Options* (March 2011), p. 139.

In: Federal Programs and Policies for Highways   ISBN: 978-1-62257-755-2
Editors: E.D. Campbell and E.Sanchez © 2013 Nova Science Publishers, Inc.

Chapter 3

THE ROLE OF THE ENVIRONMENTAL REVIEW PROCESS IN FEDERALLY FUNDED HIGHWAY PROJECTS: BACKGROUND AND ISSUES FOR CONGRESS[*]

Linda Luther

SUMMARY

Under programs administered by the Department of Transportation's (DOT's) Federal Highway Administration (FHWA), certain highway and bridge projects may be eligible for federal funding. Project approval and the receipt of federal funds are conditioned on the project sponsor (e.g., a local public works or state transportation agency) meeting certain standards and complying with federal law. Activities necessary to demonstrate compliance with those requirements may be completed at various stages of project development. Although the names of each stage may vary from state to state, project development generally includes the following: planning, preliminary design and environmental review, final design and rights-of-way acquisition, construction, and facility operation and maintenance.

---

[*] This is an edited, reformatted and augmented version of the Congressional Research Service Publication, CRS Report for Congress R42479, dated April 11, 2012.

When there is debate over the time it takes to complete federal highway projects, the environmental review stage has been a primary focus of congressional attention concerning legislative options to speed project delivery. The current process includes activities necessary to demonstrate that all potential project-related impacts to the human, natural, and cultural environment are identified; effects of those impacts are taken into consideration (among other factors such as economic or community benefits) before a final decision is made; the public is included in that decision-making process; and all state, tribal, or federal compliance requirements applicable as a result of the project's environmental impacts are, or will be, met.

Compliance requirements depend on site-specific factors, including the size and scope of the project, and whether and to what degree it may affect resources such as parks, historic sites, water resources, wetlands, or urban communities. For all proposed federal-aid highway projects, however, some level of review will be required under the National Environmental Policy Act of 1969 (NEPA, 42 U.S.C. §4321 et seq.). Broadly, NEPA requires federal agencies to consider the environmental effects of an action before proceeding with it and to involve the public in the decision-making process.

The time it takes to complete the NEPA process is often the focus of debate over project delays attributable to the overall environmental review stage. However, the majority of FHWA-approved projects require limited documentation or analyses under NEPA. Further, when environmental requirements have caused project delays, requirements established under laws other than NEPA have generally been the source. This calls into question the degree to which the NEPA compliance process is a significant source of delay in completing either the environmental review process or overall project delivery. Causes of delay that have been identified are more often tied to local/state and project-specific factors, primarily local/state agency priorities, project funding levels, local opposition to a project, project complexity, or late changes in project scope. Further, approaches that have been found to expedite environmental reviews involve procedures that local and state transportation agencies may implement currently, such as efficient coordination of interagency involvement; early and continued involvement with stakeholders interested in the project; and identifying environmental issues and requirements early in project development.

Bills in the House and Senate (the American Energy and Infrastructure Jobs Act of 2012 (H.R. 7) and Moving Ahead for Progress in the 21st Century (MAP-21; S. 1813)) would reauthorize DOT programs. Both include provisions intended to expedite project delivery by changing elements of the environmental review process, particularly NEPA requirements. This report provides information on existing NEPA and environmental review requirements, particularly requirements that may be subject to change under the House and Senate proposals.

INTRODUCTION

Under programs administered by the Department of Transportation's (DOT's) Federal Highway Administration (FHWA), certain highway and bridge projects may be eligible to receive federal-aid funding.[1] As a condition of receiving those funds, a project sponsor (e.g., a local or state transportation agency) must meet certain standards and requirements applicable to activities completed at every stage of project development. Although the names of those stages may vary somewhat from state to state, those stages generally include initial project planning, preliminary design/engineering and environmental review, final design and rights-of-way acquisition, construction, and facility operation and maintenance.

Each stage of project development is initiated and completed largely at the state or local level, with FHWA having ultimate responsibility for ensuring that individual projects comply with requirements applicable to federal-aid highways.[2] Also, each development stage involves a range of activities that will affect the time it takes to deliver the project. Required elements of the preliminary design and environmental review stage will vary by project, but generally include processes necessary to identify and demonstrate compliance with environmental requirements applicable to that project.

When there is debate over the time it takes to complete federally funded highway projects,[3] particularly debate over activities that may expedite or delay project delivery, various elements of the environmental review stage of project development have been the focus of attention. However, whether or the degree to which elements of that process may delay projects is unclear.[4]

The two most recent laws authorizing DOT programs included require-ments intended to expedite the environmental review process that focused primarily on procedures necessary to demonstrate compliance with the National Environmental Policy Act of 1969 (NEPA, 42 U.S.C. §4321 et seq.).[5] Current legislation to authorize DOT programs in the House and the Senate (the American Energy and Infrastructure Jobs Act of 2012 (H.R. 7) and Moving Ahead for Progress in the 21st Century (MAP-21; S. 1813)) also include provisions intended to expedite project delivery that focus primarily on the NEPA process.[6]

Despite the focus on the NEPA process, it is unclear whether or how changes to that process would result in faster highway project delivery. Available evidence regarding potential causes of project delays associated with environmental compliance is largely anecdotal and specific to unique, individual projects. Still, that evidence, while limited, points to issues or requirements apart from NEPA as more common causes of project delays.

This report identifies issues relevant to the debate over the role of the environmental review process in transportation project delivery. It identifies social and environmental issues that led Congress to enact the range of requirements that now make up the environmental review process, as well as selected requirements applicable to its implementation (particularly NEPA requirements). The report also identifies complexities in tying the environmental review process to federal-aid highway project delivery time. In particular, it identifies issues that make it difficult to determine the time it takes to complete the project development process, in general, or individual stages of development (e.g., activities related explicitly to environmental reviews); or to identify root causes of project delays tied to specific elements of the environmental review process. This report also discusses various approaches identified by transportation stakeholders as those that have expedited the environmental review process and overall project delivery.

Information and issues in this report were selected to help Members of Congress and their staff understand the NEPA compliance process as well as additional environmental compliance requirements that may be affected by H.R. 7 and MAP-21.

BACKGROUND AND OVERVIEW OF ISSUES

Activities that may take place during the environmental review process and how that process is implemented will vary from project to project, from state to state. The environmental review process does not involve compliance with a single federal compliance requirement. It involves processes necessary to demonstrate compliance with a potentially wide array of requirements applicable to projects approved under the Federal-aid Highways program. Broadly, for federally funded highway projects, it involves two separate, but related processes—preparing appropriate documentation required under

NEPA; and identifying and demonstrating compliance with any additional state, tribal, or federal environmental requirements applicable to that project.

For a given project, how NEPA and other environmental compliance requirements must be demonstrated will largely depend on the degree to which the proposed project would have adverse effects on communities, natural or cultural resources (e.g., wetlands, endangered species habitat, historic sites, parks, or recreation areas), or special status land (e.g., farmland, floodplains, or coastal zones). Compliance with those requirements may include obtaining a permit, approval, study, or some level of analysis or consultation from an agency outside DOT.

NEPA was intended, in part, to ensure that federal agencies would consider the environmental impacts of an action among other factors (e.g., economic or community benefits) in the federal decision-making process. NEPA has two primary aims—to assure that federal agencies consider the environmental effects of their actions *before* proceeding with them and to involve the public in the decision-making process.

NEPA does not require an agency to elevate environmental concerns above other factors in the overall federal decision-making process. If the adverse environmental effects of a proposed action are adequately identified and evaluated, an agency is not constrained by NEPA from deciding that other project benefits outweigh the environmental costs and moving forward with the action. In contrast, other requirements applicable to federal-aid highways *may* dictate or somehow affect the outcome of a project decision. For example, other federal laws may require the selected project alternative to be the one with the least impact to a particular resource, prohibit FHWA approval of a project alternative that uses certain resources, require certain mitigation measures to limit a project's impacts, or require that certain activities take place in accordance with certain criteria (e.g., as specified in a permit or approval).

Environmental Reviews and Project Delays

Required elements of the environmental review process, particularly compliance with NEPA, will have an effect on project development. For example, before DOT can approve a project and allow final project design, property acquisition, or project construction to proceed, the project sponsor must appropriately document compliance with NEPA and complete any investigation, review, or consultation necessary to demonstrate compliance with other applicable environmental requirements. Further, it is DOT policy to use the NEPA compliance process as a mechanism to balance transportation decision making by taking into account the potential impacts on the human and natural environment and the public's need for safe and efficient transportation.[7]

State and local transportation agency officials and other stakeholders with an interest in transportation improvement generally acknowledge that elements of the environmental review process provide important protections to the human, cultural, and natural environment. However, those officials also sometimes argue that completing the process can be difficult and time-consuming. Some have argued, for example, that the time it takes to complete required NEPA documentation and supporting analysis or to obtain required input or approval from outside agencies can delay completion of federally funded transportation projects.

It is generally not disputed that the time it takes to complete the environmental review process for federally funded highway projects can take months or even years. What is unclear is the degree to which elements of the environmental review process directly or routinely delay project delivery. Determining the time it takes to complete activities associated with the environmental review process, or delays directly attributable to those activities, is difficult for several reasons including, but not limited to:

- **Limits to available data.** There is no centralized source of data regarding highway project delivery. States generally do not track project development time from planning to construction. States generally do not attempt to isolate elements of the environmental review process, which may overlap with preliminary project planning, design, or engineering activities. Further, there is no standard measure for determining when a project or the environmental review process, in particular, is completed "quickly" or would be considered "delayed."
- **The influence of local factors on project delivery.** The environmental review process may start, stop, and restart for reasons unrelated to environmental issues. Local and state issues have been shown to have the most significant influence on whether a project moves forward relatively quickly or takes longer than anticipated. Those issues include the project's level of priority among others proposed in the state; changes in funding availability; and local

controversy or opposition to the project (which may or may not be connected to environmental issues).

- **The variation in project type and complexity.** The wide range of projects approved under programs administered by FHWA (e.g., bridge repair versus major new highway construction) do not easily allow an "apples to apples" comparison of the time it takes to complete the environmental review process or factors that may delay it. Anecdotal evidence regarding projects identified as "delayed" have involved multiple, complex causes of delay (including local issues) unique to *that* project, not a single cause that may be commonly applicable to other projects.

- **Variation among state requirements and implementation processes.** The effect of requirements under federal law may be difficult to isolate since local, state, or tribal requirements and procedures will also affect how environmental compliance requirements are implemented. State DOTs implement their project delivery process differently, depending on factors specific to their state and its needs. For example, some states may implement unique design and contracting processes that expedite project delivery that other states do not.

- **Time "saved" cannot be gauged.** Depending on the scope and complexity of the project, more time spent addressing environmental issues in the project planning and preliminary design stage may result in faster completion of final design and project construction (when delays may require actions that take more time and money to address). Time may also be saved when adverse project impacts that could lead to local opposition to the project are identified and addressed during the early stages of project development.

Challenges to Tying Project Delays to NEPA Compliance

Transportation agency officials and project sponsors have broadly identified environmental compliance requirements as a common source of frustration in completing the project development process. However, limits to and contradiction in available data make it difficult to clearly identify specific causes of delay that are directly and routinely attributable to specific elements of environmental compliance. Identifying a distinct root cause of a delay will arguably be necessary before effective "solutions" (procedures that would result in faster project delivery) can be identified. That is, knowing *that* a delay occurred may be irrelevant if it is not determined *why* the delay occurred. An understanding of *why* is useful in identifying a solution that directly addresses a problem's underlying cause.

Determining why a project was delayed may be difficult or may be attributable to multiple, interrelated factors. Generally, the more complex the project, the more complex the potential cause(s) of delay. For example, compared to a maintenance or repair project, a major new construction project will require more extensive review, documentation, or analysis to demonstrate compliance with NEPA and other applicable environmental requirements. However, the following factors call into question the degree to which NEPA alone is a significant source of project delay in overall project development:

- **The majority of projects require limited review under NEPA.** The majority of FHWA-approved projects (approximately 96%) involve no significant environmental impacts and, hence, require limited documentation, analysis, or review under NEPA.
- **Compliance with DOT's "NEPA regulations" extends beyond what is required under NEPA.** DOT's "Environmental Impact and Related Procedures"[8] prescribe the policies and procedures to ensure that FHWA-approved projects will comply with NEPA as well as requirements established under Title 23 applicable to Federal-aid Highways (e.g., provisions applicable to the consideration of adverse economic, social, and environmental effects (under §109(h)), public hearings (§128), and preservation of parklands (§138)).
- **The NEPA compliance process is used to demonstrate compliance with all applicable environmental review requirements.** It is DOT policy that any investigation, review, or consultation necessary to demonstrate compliance withapplicable environmental requirements be completed within the context of the NEPA process. This use of NEPA as an "umbrella" compliance process can blurthe distinction between what is required under NEPA and what is required under separate authority.

Transportation agency officials asked to identify sources of frustration or delay in completing the environmental review process most commonly cite compliance requirements applicable to the protection of parklands, historic sites, wetlands, or threatened or endangered species. The potential root cause of delay in complying with those requirements could be attributable to a wide range of project-specific factors (e.g., incomplete permit applications, challenges in obtaining multiple approvals or permits for a complex project, or disagreement with a resource agency over appropriate methods to mitigate project impacts).

Both existing law and regulations implementing NEPA include explicit directives and requirements intended to streamline the NEPA process. Included among those requirements are procedures intended to coordinate efficient agency interaction and cooperation, reduce NEPA-related paperwork and duplication of effort (e.g., documentation and analysis that may be required by similar state, tribal, or federal requirements or from one stage of project development to the next), and integrate the consideration of environmental compliance issues in a project's planning stage. Barriers to efficiently implementing existing requirements may be project-specific or involve issues that may be difficult to address by simply amending or eliminating existing federal requirements.

This is not to suggest that there are not instances where preparation of documentation and analysis required under NEPA is not time-consuming or may contribute to delays in project delivery. However, it is unclear whether or what additional federal requirements may be implemented to expedite the NEPA process. Conversely, it is not clear whether the elimination of certain NEPA-specific requirements may expedite project delivery or would alter the framework for coordinating an already complex compliance process, resulting in additional project delay. For a given project, whether changes to the NEPA process might result in faster project delivery will likely depend on the project's scope and complexity; the degree to which it is affected by "local" factors (e.g., state funding or project priorities); and compliance requirements applicable to the project, in addition to those under NEPA.

HIGHWAY CONSTRUCTION IMPACTS THAT LED TO THE CURRENT PROCESS

To understand why a complex array of requirements may apply to highway projects, it is useful to understand the social and environmental concerns that led Congress to enact the various laws that now form the framework of the environmental review process. Each requirement included within that process represents past efforts by Congress to minimize adverse impacts from federally funded highway projects or to minimize adverse impacts to certain communities or resources that Congress identified as needing some level of protection.

The current debate over the environmental review process frequently centers around the effect that completion of that process has on project delivery. The debate rarely recognizes the issues that led Congress to enact the requirements that now make up that process. Requirements included within the environmental review process, and procedures to demonstrate compliance with them, have evolved over the past 50 years. However, many of the requirements that are subject to particular scrutiny today were enacted between 1966 and 1972.

During the 1950s and 1960s, the public was becoming increasingly aware of and concerned about the impacts that human activity were having on the environment. Increasing attention turned to the effect that federally funded programs and projects were having on the human, cultural, and natural environment. One federal program that generated particular concern was the development and construction of the Interstate Highway System.

The Federal-Aid Highway Act of 1956 (P.L. 84-627) authorized and provided revenue sources for the construction of the National System of Interstate and Defense Highways (commonly known as the Interstate Highway System, Interstate System, or the Interstate). The Interstate System is a network of limited-access roads including freeways, highways, and expressways forming part of the National Highway System of the United States.[9] Construction of the Interstate System took approximately 35 years and resulted in a network of roads and bridges that currently includes over 45,000 miles of rural highways, suburban and urban freeways, and bridges.[10]

Although the connection of rural, urban, and suburban communities resulted in a host of economic and cultural benefits, construction of the Interstate System also brought certain adverse impacts to both the human and natural environment.

Those impacts were seen particularly in the construction of the urban freeways. Planning for such projects often involved locating freeways within available open space or where land acquisition costs were relatively low. "Available open space" often meant historic sites, parks, or recreation areas. Adverse impacts to those resources from highway projects drew increased attention from newly formed stakeholder groups with an interest in environmental protection and historic preservation.

Project planning that involved lower land acquisition costs often meant property acquisitions in densely populated, working-class or high-poverty neighborhoods.

Resulting urban freeway projects had a disproportionate impact on the urban poor. One such example involved a segment of I-95 north of Miami. The route selected by local transportation officials cut through the inner-city community of Overtown, a once-thriving African-American community known as the "Harlem of the South." A 2009 FHWA report discussing lessons learned in complying with environmental requirements describes the project as follows:

> In 1957, the Overtown community was almost decimated by the development of the I-95 and I-395 freeways. The constructed roadway had a disastrous impact on the economic and social structure of the community. The community continues to shoulder the lingering effects of those negative impacts, and as a result there is also persistent anger towards and distrust of [the Florida Department of Transportation].[11]

Opposition to other urban freeway projects led to "freeway revolts" spearheaded by newly established environmental and social justice groups.[12] Freeway revolts took place in cities like Baltimore, Boston, Los Angeles, New Orleans, New York, Reno, and San Francisco. As a result, a significant number of projects were abandoned or significantly scaled back due to widespread public opposition, especially by those whose neighborhoods would be disrupted or who would displaced by the proposed freeways.

ELEMENTS OF THE ENVIRONMENTAL REVIEW PROCESS

By the mid to late 1960s, Congress began to enact legislation intended to address the growing public concern over projects implemented under the Federal-aid Highways program. During that period, Congress also enacted legislation in response to increasing awareness and concern over the impacts of all federal actions—not just federal highway projects. Also during the 1960s and into the 1970s Congress began to enact a wide range of laws intended to identify, prohibit, control, or mitigate adverse impacts of human activities to specific community, natural, or cultural resources that Congress identified as in need of certain protection.

This report identifies and summarizes requirements that have been identified as those most commonly applicable to federally funded highway projects.

Requirements Applicable to Federal-aid Highways

FHWA is prohibited from approving a project for funding under the
Federal-aid Highway program until the project sponsor demonstrates that the
proposed project will comply with all applicable federal, tribal, and state
requirements. To the extent possible, compliance with any requirements that
apply to a project, as a result of that project's effect on the human and natural
environment, must be appropriately documented and demonstrated during the
environmental review stage of project development.

Requirements specific to Federal-aid Highways include a host of
standards, procedures, and conditions applicable to the various stages of
project development. Several requirements (applicable primarily to activities
that take place during the project planning, preliminary design, and
environmental review phases of development) reflect concern over the effects
of urban freeway construction (discussed above), including the following:

- **Directive to establish guidelines to assure consideration of adverse
  project impacts (23 U.S.C. §109(h)).** Directed DOT to establish
  guidelines to assure that possible adverse, economic, social, and
  environmental effects of proposed highway projects and project
  locations were fully considered during project development, and that
  final project decisions be made in the best overall public interest,
  taking into consideration the costs of eliminating or minimizing
  adverse effects to air, noise, and water pollution; destruction or
  disruption of man-made and natural resources; aesthetic values,
  community cohesion, and the availability of public facilities and
  services; adverse employment effects, and tax and property value
  losses; and injurious displacement of people, businesses, and farms.
- **Directive to establish noise standards (23 U.S.C. §109(i)).** Directed
  DOT to establish standards for highway noise levels compatible with
  different land uses. DOT cannot approve plans and specifications for
  any proposed federal-aid project unless it includes adequate measures
  to implement those noise standards. As implemented under DOT
  regulations, a project may be required to demonstrate compliance with
  applicable standards through an analysis of traffic noise impacts and,
  when necessary, to implement noise abatement measures.
- **Public hearings requirements (23 U.S.C. §128).** For a proposed
  project bypassing or going through any city, town, or village, a state
  transportation department is required to certify that it held or afforded

the opportunity for public hearings; considered the economic and social effects of the project location, and its impact on the environment; and considered the consistency of the project with local planning goals and objectives.

- **Preservation of parklands requirements (23 U.S.C. §138).** More commonly referred to as "Section 4(f)"[13] requirements, DOT is prohibited from approving a project that uses publicly owned (local, state, or federal) parks and recreation areas, wildlife and waterfowl refuges, and publicly or privately owned historic sites of national, state, or local significance. DOT may approve a project that uses a 4(f) resource only if there is no prudent and feasible alternative to do otherwise, and that use includes all possible planning to minimize harm to the resource.

Of the requirements specifically applicable to Federal-aid Highways, the preservation of parklands requirements may have the greatest effect on highway project development and delivery. Projects that would use a 4(f) resource require an evaluation analyzing project alternatives (including location and design shifts) that avoid the resource.[14] To be approved by FHWA, the evaluation must show that alternatives that would not use the resource would result in "truly unique problems," resulting in costs or community disruption of extraordinary magnitude. This test is often referred to as the "Overton Park Criteria," after a court case in the 1970s in Memphis, TN.[15] In approving the use of a 4(f) resource, FHWA must also consider the significance and importance of the resource itself.

SAFETEA amended Section 138 to allow for the use of a 4(f) resource if that use can be proven to have *de minimis* impacts to the resource.[16] Generally, *de minimis* impacts would result from the use of minor amounts of a particular resource. Such a determination requires concurrence from an official with jurisdiction over the resource. For example, for a transportation project adjacent to a publicly owned park, recreation area, or wildlife and waterfowl refuge, FHWA would be required to consult with, as appropriate, agencies within the Department of the Interior (e.g., the U.S. Fish and Wildlife Service, National Park Service, or the Bureau of Indian Affairs) or state or local park authorities. For historic sites, a *de minimis* impacts determination must be based on criteria established under the National Historic Preservation Act applicable to uses that will have no "adverse effect" on the site (16 U.S.C. §470f). The determination must receive concurrence from the State Historic

Preservation Officer (SHPO) and, if appropriate, the Advisory Council on Historic Preservation (ACHP).

Compared to other environmental requirements likely applicable to federal-aid highway projects, Section 4(f) is unique in its limits on the use of a protected resource. Most requirements intended to protect communities or specific natural or cultural resources allow for adverse project impacts if those impacts are sufficiently identified and considered in the decision-making process. Some requirements may specify that a project implement certain mitigation measures or be implemented in accordance with an approval or permit from an agency responsible for protecting that resource. An outright prohibition on the use of a particular resource, except for *de minimis* impacts or under extraordinary conditions, is not common to other environmental requirements.

Requirements Applicable to "Federal Actions"

In the 1960s Congress debated legislative options to address potential adverse impacts associated with federal actions. An action may be deemed "federal" based on the role that a federal agency plays in a project's approval or funding. A project funded under the Federal-aid Highways program would generally be considered a federal action. Two laws applicable specifically to federal actions that significantly affect the environmental review process for highway project development are NEPA and the National Historic Preservation Act (16 U.S.C. §470, et seq.).

As discussed previously, NEPA has two primary aims—to require federal agencies to consider the environmental impacts of a project and to give the public a meaningful opportunity to learn about and comment on the proposed project *before* a final decision is made. It is a procedural statute. That is, NEPA requires federal agencies to implement procedures to ensure that environmental impacts of a project are included among, but not elevated above, other factors considered during the federal decision-making process. If the adverse environmental impacts of the proposed action are adequately identified and evaluated, the agency is not constrained by NEPA from deciding that other benefits (e.g., community and economic benefits) outweigh the environmental costs and moving forward with the action. (The NEPA compliance process is discussed under "Demonstrating Compliance with NEPA.")

The National Historic Preservation Act (NHPA) declared a national policy of historic preservation to protect districts, sites, buildings, structures, and objects significant to American architecture, history, archaeology, and culture. NHPA did not mandate preservation of historic resources or prohibit adverse impacts to them, but Section 106 requires all federal agencies to consider the impacts of a proposal prior to taking any action that may affect a site included in, or eligible for inclusion on, the National Register of Historic Places.

NHPA also requires federal agencies to afford the Advisory Council on Historic Preservation (an independent federal agency created by the law) a reasonable opportunity to comment on federal actions that would affect properties on or eligible for inclusion on the National Register of Historic Places. For federally funded highway projects, FHWA must consult with the Advisory Council or the designated SHPO to determine project impacts to historic sites and potential ways to mitigate those impacts.

There are similarities between requirements established under Section 4(f) and Section 106, but also important differences between the statutes. Like NEPA, Section 106 establishes a procedural requirement that directs all federal agencies only to consider project impacts on certain resources. Section 4(f) applies only to DOT projects and prohibits the use of certain resources for those projects, except under certain conditions.

Additional federal laws and executive orders apply explicitly to federal actions that affect certain resources or communities. For example, a federally funded highway project may require compliance with additional requirements applicable to federal actions if that project may:

- involve the acquisition, rehabilitation, or demolition of real property that will displace persons from their homes, businesses, or farms as protected under the Uniform Relocation Assistance and Real Property Acquisition Act of 1970 (42 U.S.C. §4601, et seq., more commonly referred to as the Uniform Act);
- affect wetlands or floodplains pursuant to Executive Order 11990 or Executive Order 11988, respectively;
- convert farmland to nonagricultural uses pursuant to the Farmland Protection Policy Act of 1981 (7 U.S.C. §4201 et seq.);
- cause disproportionately high and adverse impacts on minority and low-income populations with respect to human health and the environment pursuant to Executive Order 12898; or

- affect human remains and cultural material of Native American and Hawaiian groups pursuant to the Native American Grave Protection and Repatriation Act (25 U.S.C. §3001 et seq.).

Requirements Applicable to Certain Resources

In addition to requirements applicable to federal-aid highways, specifically, and federal actions, in general, Congress has enacted a host of individual statutes intended to protect certain natural, environmental, and cultural resources from human-induced activities. A potentially long list of federal compliance requirements *could* apply to a given highway or bridge project, but requirements that will *actually* apply to a project will be limited by site-specific conditions and the degree to which the proposed project may affect protected resources. Broadly, highway projects may be subject to requirements intended to identify, minimize, or control adverse impacts to:

- **Land**—including land use that may affect the habitat of threatened or endangered plant and animal species, migratory birds, archaeological sites, and land designated as a national trail or national wilderness; and
- **Water resources or water quality**—including projects that may affect wetlands, aquatic ecosystems, navigable waters (e.g., rivers, streams, harbors), floodplains, coastal zones, or designated "wild and scenic" rivers, or projects that may affect water quality (e.g., discharge pollutants into U.S. waters).[17]

For a given federally funded highway project, compliance with a number of federal, state, or tribal regulations intended to identify, control, mitigate, or minimize project impacts to land and water resources may be required. Specific compliance requirements will depend on standards or regulatory requirements of that law and the degree to which the proposed project may adversely affect that resource.

Depending on those factors, project development and implementation may require some level of consultation, analysis, or approval from an agency with jurisdiction over the resource. For example, a highway or bridge project that results in pollutants being discharged into wetlands, rivers, or streams or that may affect navigable waterways or harbors likely will require project development be completed in accordance with provisions established under the Clean Water Act or the Rivers and Harbors Act. Pursuant to those laws, the selection of a particular project alternative may require a permit or certification from the Army Corps of Engineers (the Corps), the Environmental Protection Agency (EPA), the United States Coast Guard, or a state or tribal water quality control agency.

IMPLEMENTING THE ENVIRONMENTAL REVIEW PROCESS

The individual requirements discussed above were enacted by Congress after a particular concern arose or need was identified. For an individual project, several requirements involving similar compliance directives could apply. For example, depending on its impacts, a project may be subject to different public hearing or notification requirements under separate federal regulatory or statutory requirements. The environmental review process is intended to function as the mechanism under which potentially duplicative requirements are identified and coordinated (including duplicative state or tribal requirements).

Specifically, it is DOT policy that, to the fullest extent possible, any investigation, review, and consultation necessary to demonstrate environmental compliance be coordinated as a single process. The environmental review process is that single process. It forms the framework under which *all* applicable compliance requirements intended to protect the human, natural, or cultural environment are identified and demonstrated. Further, the NEPA compliance process forms the framework for completing the environmental review process.

In the past, suggestions made by transportation stakeholders to expedite project delivery, as well as legislative options proposed by some Members of Congress, have focused on requirements established specifically under NEPA. However, examples of individual projects delayed by environmental requirements more often involve issues associated with environmental compliance obligations established under separate state or federal requirements. In identifying and determining the potential effectiveness of nationally applicable approaches to expedite the environmental review process, it is necessary to distinguish between what is required explicitly under NEPA versus other federal environmental requirements.

Demonstrating Compliance with NEPA

The Council on Environmental Quality (CEQ) promulgated regulations implementing NEPA that were broadly applicable to all federal agencies.[18] CEQ required each federal agency to develop its own NEPA procedures specific to typical classes of actions undertaken by that agency.[19] In 1987, DOT promulgated "Environmental Impact and Related Procedures."[20] Those regulations prescribe the policies and procedures for FHWA to implement NEPA as it may apply to federally funded highway projects. They also include procedures necessary to ensure compliance with environmental requirements established under Title 23 applicable to Federal-aid Highways (e.g., procedures necessary to demonstrate compliance with requirements applicable to economic, social, and environmental effects, public hearings, and preservation of parklands (Section 4(f))). DOT's regulations have been revised periodically in accordance with legislative directives from Congress and to reflect court decisions applicable to DOT's implementation of both the NEPA process and its other environmental compliance obligations. Most recently, the regulations were modified to reflect the new environmental review process established under SAFETEA.

Identifying the Appropriate NEPA Document

For a given highway project that receives funding or approval under Federal-aid Highways programs, compliance with NEPA is demonstrated in the "NEPA document." Requirements that define the various categories of NEPA document and required elements of each are found in the NEPA regulations promulgated by both CEQ and DOT.

Transportation projects vary in type, size, complexity, and potential to affect the environment. To account for the variability of potential project impacts, NEPA regulations establish three basic "classes of action" that dictate how NEPA compliance will be documented and implemented. Determining the appropriate NEPA document and level of environmental review and analysis necessary for that document is dependent upon the answer to the following question: "Will the proposed action have any significant environmental impact?" Answers to that question, and the corresponding NEPA documents, are as follows:

- **Yes.** Those projects require an Environmental Impact Statement (EIS) followed by a final Record of Decision (ROD).

- **Maybe.** When the significance of a project's impacts is not clear, an Environmental Assessment (EA) must be prepared to determine whether an EIS is necessary or a Finding of No Significant Impact (FONSI) is appropriate.
- **No.** Those projects are categorically excluded from the requirement to prepare an EIS or EA; as such, those projects are generally referred to as Categorical Exclusions (CEs or CATEX).

Pursuant to NEPA's aims, an evaluation of environmental impacts is required prior to commitment of federal resources. To meet that requirement, preparation of the NEPA document may begin in the project planning stage, but must be completed within the preliminary design and environmental review stage of project development. Generally, subsequent stages of project development (final design activities, property acquisition, or project construction) cannot proceed until the necessary NEPA document is complete and approved by FHWA.

FHWA-Approved Projects by NEPA Class of Action

Major highway projects that require an EIS are the most studied and discussed when there is debate over the time it takes to complete the NEPA process. Further, past legislative efforts to expedite the NEPA process have focused primarily on the NEPA process as it applies to EIS preparation. However, FHWA data from 1998 to 2007 show that approximately 4% of federal-aid highway projects approved under programs administered by FHWA required an EIS. Projects processed as a CE or with an EA/FONSI accounted for approximately 96% (see **Figure 1**).

More recent FHWA data illustrate a similar proportion of major new projects and smaller maintenance/rehabilitation projects. In FY2009, of the approximately 55,043 miles of roadway projects receiving federal-aid highway funds, approximately 50,166 miles (91%) involved reconstruction projects with no added roadway capacity, restoration and rehabilitation activities, or road resurfacing (i.e., projects likely to be processed as CEs). Approximately 4,877 miles of road construction projects involved new construction, relocation, or reconstruction with added capacity (i.e., projects likely to require preparation of an EA or EIS).[21]

In addition to representing a small number of overall projects, few projects currently being developed require an EIS. As of November 18, 2011, 10 states had no active projects that involved EIS preparation, 12 states and the District of Columbia and Puerto Rico were preparing 1, and 18 states were preparing between 2 and 5 (illustrated in **Figure 2**). Further, a significant number of active EISs (68 of 175 or 39%) were being prepared in just five states— California, Texas, North Carolina, Florida, and New York.

While projects requiring an EIS represent a small proportion of total projects and a small number of active projects being developed in each state, they are more likely to be high-profile, complex projects that affect sizeable populations and take years, even decades, from planning to construction. They may cost millions, or even hundreds of millions, of dollars. For example, data from 1998 to 2007 regarding FHWA funding allocation show that while projects processed as CEs generally represent 90% of projects approved, those projects accounted for approximately 76% of FHWA program funds. Over that period, projects requiring an EIS accounted for approximately 4% of the total projects approved, but 12% of allocated program funds (see **Figure 3**).

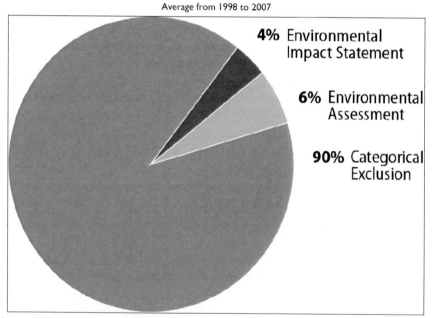

Source: Congressional Research Service, based on data available from FHWA's "Streamlining/Stewardship: Performance Reporting" website at http://www. environment.fhwa.dot.gov/strmlng/projectgraphs.asp/.

Figure 1. FHWA-Approved Projects—By NEPA Class of Action.

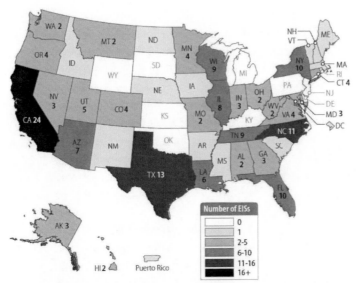

Source: Congressional Research Service, based on FHWA's list of Active and Inactive Environmental Impact Statements (EISs) as of November 18, 2011, available on the agency's "NEPA and Project Development" website at http://www. environment.fhwa.dot.gov/projdev/active_eis.asp.

Figure 2. Active FHWA Projects Requiring an EIS in Each State.

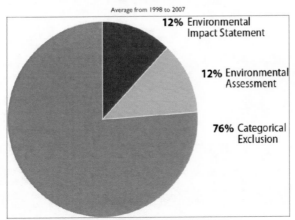

Source: Congressional Research Service, based on data available on FHWA's "Streamlining/Stewardship: Performance Reporting" website, http://www. environment.fhwa.dot.gov/strmlng/projectgraphs.asp/.

Figure 3. Percentage of FHWA Program Funding Allocation by NEPA Class of Action.

While a project requiring an EIS will likely cost more than a project processed as a CE, there is not necessarily a direct relationship between a project's cost and its level of environmental impacts. For example, it cannot be stated that projects that cost over $1 million, or even $10 million, will require an EIS. This point is illustrated by reviewing FHWA's list of "Major Projects," defined to include those expected to receive over $500 million in federal assistance.[22] Included on FHWA's list of currently active major projects are several that are being processed as CEs or with an approved FONSI.[23] For example, the "Loop 12/State Highway 35E Corridor" project in the Dallas-Fort Worth, TX, area is described as a reconstruction and widening project estimated to cost $1.6 billion. Project letting for that project began after approval of an EA/FONSI. Also included on the list is the "I-595 Corridor Improvements Project." That project, determined to be a CE, will add reversible lanes and involve major interchange improvements along 10.5 miles of the I-595 corridor in Florida. It is estimated to cost $1.8 billion.

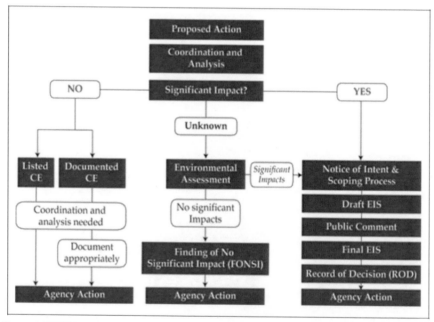

Source: FHWA guidance document, *Integrating Road Safety into NEPA Analysis: A Primer for Safety and Environmental Professionals*, in the "FHWA Environmental Toolkit," available at http://www.environment.fhwa.dot.gov/ projdev/pd6rs_primer_sec2.asp.

Figure 4. NEPA Decision-Making Process.

Selected Requirements for Each Category of NEPA Document

Each NEPA document (EIS, EA, and CE) must include certain required elements (see **Figure 4**). That is, the NEPA document must show that environmental impacts were considered as part of the federal decision-making process, not a paperwork exercise to document impacts from a project after a decision was made.

Requirements applicable to each element of each NEPA document, and how DOT requires an applicant for federal funds to demonstrate compliance with each element, largely evolved in the 20 years after NEPA was enacted. Those requirements are reflected in both CEQ and DOT regulations implementing NEPA. The evolution of the NEPA compliance process was also influenced by the courts. For example, the courts played a prominent role in determining issues such as what constitutes "significant" impacts, who must prepare an EIS, at what point an EIS must be prepared, and how adverse comments from agencies should be handled. Changes to required elements of the NEPA process, applicable to projects funded under DOT programs, are also made by Congress.

Selected requirements applicable to each category of NEPA document, including requirements established under SAFETEA, are discussed below.

Categorical Exclusion (CE) Determinations

As discussed above, projects processed as CEs represent the greatest proportion of projects approved for federal-aid highway funds. DOT defines CEs as actions that, based on past experience with similar actions, do not individually or collectively have a significant impact on any natural, cultural, recreational, historic, or other resource, or involve significant air, noise, or water quality impacts; and that will *not*

- induce significant impacts to planned growth or land use for the area;
- require the relocation of significant numbers of people;
- have significant impacts on travel patterns; or
- otherwise, either individually or cumulatively, have any significant environmental impacts.[24]

A project may meet these criteria, but still involve "unusual circumstances" that would require FHWA to ensure that a CE designation is appropriate. Unusual circumstances applicable to federally funded highway projects include substantial project controversy on environmental grounds; a significant impact on properties protected under Section 4(f) or Section 106 of the National Historic Preservation Act (NHPA); or inconsistencies with any federal, state, or local requirements relating to the environmental aspects of the action.[25]

DOT identifies two groups of surface transportation projects that would likely meet the CE criteria (absent any unusual circumstances applicable to the project). The first group includes specific actions that meet criteria applicable to CEs.[26] DOT has determined that these projects (presented in **Table 1**) will likely result in insignificant environmental impacts because they either do not involve or directly lead to construction or involve minor construction.

A proposed action included in this list may or may not require an applicant for federal funds to submit supporting documentation to FHWA. Necessary paperwork could range from a simple checklist to substantial documentation. The extent of paperwork or supporting documentation is directly related to the extent of the impacts and necessary analysis of those impacts. For example, construction of a bicycle path or installation of traffic signals in a historic district may require some level of compliance with Section 106 of the NHPA or Section 4(f).

The second group of CEs includes actions that past DOT experience has shown to have substantial, but generally not "significant," effects.[27] For this group, DOT regulations include "examples" of actions commonly approved by FHWA that may meet the regulatory definition of a CE (presented in **Table 2**). Such projects require the project sponsor to provide FHWA with documentation to confirm that the project does not involve "unusual circumstances" resulting in significant environmental impacts. Unlike specifically "listed CEs" (**Table 1**), the potential universe of "documented CEs" is not limited to projects identified by DOT. Instead, FHWA may approve a CE designation for any action as long as documentation is provided that demonstrates the project meets the regulatory definition of a CE.

Although they are excluded from the requirement to prepare an EIS or EA, CEs are sometimes incorrectly identified as being exempt from NEPA or having *no* environmental impacts. No *significant* environmental impact *under* NEPA does not mean the project has *no other* regulated environmental impacts. For example, to demonstrate that a project meets both the CE criteria and will comply with other environmental requirements, state DOTs routinely gather information regarding a CE's potential to

- involve work that requires highway traffic or construction noise abatement;

- be located within certain limits of a sole source aquifer or alter stream flow;
- involve the acquisition of more than minor amounts of temporary or permanent right-of-way;
- require a Section 4(f) evaluation or "an opinion of adverse effect" under Section 106 of NHPA;
- involve commercial or residential displacement;
- involve work in wetlands that would require a permit from the Corps; or
- be constructed in a county that lists federal threatened and endangered species.

A project may involve any one or more of these (or other) activities that will have some effect on the human or natural environment, yet have environmental impacts that do not rise to the level of "significant" under NEPA. However, the threshold of significant impacts is primarily relevant to NEPA compliance. Other laws intended to protect or mitigate impacts to natural or cultural resources will have their own compliance thresholds applicable to *that* law. FHWA approval of a project processed as a CE may be delayed if the project sponsor does not realize that its proposed project may be subject to compliance requirements in addition to NEPA.

Within its responsibilities to oversee the Federal-aid Highway program, FHWA typically establishes procedures with each state DOT regarding CE review and approval. In a given state, "listed CEs" generally require minimal documentation before FHWA approval. NEPA review for those projects would be included as part of FHWA's project oversight and approval obligations established under Title 23. For "documented CEs," FHWA either reviews the NEPA documentation as part of the project development process and any agreed-upon procedures as part of the project review and approval, or the state DOT does this review in accordance with a formal programmatic CE agreement established between FHWA and the state DOT.

A programmatic CE agreement sets forth specific project circumstances for which a CE could be processed, and maintains FHWA oversight and responsibility for the NEPA determination. A programmatic approach involves establishing a streamlined process for handling routine environmental requirements, commonly applicable to specific types of project (e.g., bridge maintenance or road resurfacing activities). It allows for repetitive actions to be considered on a programmatic basis rather than project by project. Established on a local, regional, or statewide basis, a programmatic CE may establish procedures for consultation, review, and compliance with one or more federal laws. FHWA suggests that, to the extent possible, state DOTs take a programmatic approach to CE determinations.

Table 1. Federally Funded Highway Projects Specifically Listed as CEs

Non-construction activities (e.g., planning, technical studies, or research activities).	Emergency repairs after a natural disaster or catastrophic failure.
Installing fencing, signs, pavement markings, small passenger shelters, and traffic signals that involve no substantial land acquisition or traffic disruption.	Deploying electronic, photonic, communication, or information processing systems to improve system efficiency or safety.
Altering a facility to make it accessible to elderly and handicapped persons.	Landscaping activities.
Implementing ridesharing programs.	Improving existing rest areas or truck weigh stations.
Scenic easement acquisition.	Installing noise barriers.
Activities in a state highway safety plan.	Constructing bicycle or pedestrian lanes or facilities.

Source: Congressional Research Service, taken from actions listed at 23 C.F.R. §771.117(c).

Table 2. Examples of FHWA-Approved Projects
That May be Classified as a CE

Actions That May Be Designated a CE with Appropriate Documentation and FHWA Approval	
Highway modernization through resurfacing, restoration, rehabilitation, or reconstruction.	Bridge rehabilitation, reconstruction, or replacement.
Highway safety or traffic operations improvement projects.	New truck weigh station or rest area construction.
Approval for changes in access control.	Approval for disposal of excess right-of-way or for joint or limited use of right-of-way.
Acquisition of certain preexisting railroad right-of-way.	Land acquisition for hardship or protective purposes.
Construction of transportation corridor fringe parking facilities.	

Source: Congressional Research Service, taken from examples of actions listed at 23 C.F.R. §771.117(d).

Apart from its potential to enter into programmatic CE agreements with FHWA, state DOTs may assume FHWA responsibility for CE determinations.

Pursuant to provisions in Section 6004 of SAFETEA,[28] FHWA may assign and a state DOT may assume responsibility for determining whether certain highway projects meet the CE criteria. Under that authority, a participating state would be authorized to determine all CE applicability, including determining whether proposed projects that are not specifically listed under DOT's NEPA regulations may meet the CE criteria.

States that choose to assume FHWA responsibility would be required to do so in accordance with terms and conditions established in a memorandum of understanding (MOU) between the state and FHWA.[29] States assuming federal authority are legally liable for the NEPA determination. That is, FHWA would not be liable for the NEPA determinations for CEs in states participating in the program. FHWA would be required to conduct an annual review of a participating state's process for making CE determinations. To date, three states (Alaska, California, and Utah) have requested and been assigned responsibilities under the Section 6004 program.

Environmental Impact Statements (EIS)

Projects requiring an EIS make up the smallest percentage of projects approved by FHWA, but have generated the most attention when debating NEPA's potential role in delaying highway projects. FHWA does not specifically identify actions that require an EIS. That determination must be made on a case-by-case basis. However, DOT identifies the following as examples of highway projects that normally require an EIS: a new controlled access freeway; a highway project of four or more lanes on a new location; and new construction or extension of a separate roadway for buses or high-occupancy vehicles not located within an existing highway facility.[30]

Both the steps to complete an EIS and the EIS itself include certain required elements. Each required element represents the evolution of NEPA compliance requirements—as established by CEQ and, in part, as a result of judicial interpretation of NEPA's mandate and how its procedural requirements must be implemented. Required components in EIS preparation are

- file a Notice of Intent (NOI)
- scope the environmental issues
- prepare a draft EIS
- circulate the draft EIS for comment
- prepare the final EIS
- issue a final record of decision (ROD)

The NOI serves as the formal announcement of the project to the public and to interested federal, state, tribal, and local agencies.[31] As soon as possible after, or in conjunction with, the determination that an EIS is needed, the agency is required to determine the scope of the project. During that process, the project sponsor/applicant for federal funds should determine which environmental laws, regulations, or other requirements may apply to the project. During the scoping process, routes that may pose certain challenges and could be avoided may be identified (e.g., the presence of terrain or resources that may involve potential engineering or technical problems, regulatory restrictions, or public opposition). For example, during the scoping process, a potential route or alignment may be identified that would avoid property of historical significance, endangered species habitat, or wetlands—each of which may require compliance with the NHPA, the Endangered Species Act, or the Clean Water Act, respectively.

Once the scope of the action and its environmental issues have been determined, EIS preparation can begin. Required elements of an EIS, including selected elements in DOT's NEPA regulations or FHWA policy, are summarized in **Table 3**.

The EIS is prepared in two stages, resulting in a draft and a final EIS.[32] Supplemental documents may be required in some instances. Among other requirements, the final EIS must identify the preferred project alternative; reflect an evaluation of all reasonable alternatives considered; identify and respond to public and agency comments on the draft EIS; and summarize public involvement. The final EIS should document compliance with requirements of all applicable environmental laws, executive orders, and other related requirements. If full compliance is not possible by the time the final EIS is prepared, it should reflect consultation with the appropriate agencies and provide reasonable assurance that the requirements will be met. FHWA approval of the environmental document constitutes adoption of any findings and determinations in the EIS. The ROD presents the basis for the agency's final decision and summarizes any mitigation measures that will be incorporated in the project.

Each required element of the EIS involves compliance requirements established under both NEPA and other environmental requirements. For example, a clear delineation of project purpose and need is also necessary to meet the requirements under Section 4(f), executive orders on wetlands and floodplains, and permitting requirements established under Section 404 of the Clean Water Act. Identifying the potentially affected environment and analysis of environmental consequences also demonstrate that environmental impacts are considered during, not after, the decision-making process (as required under NEPA), but also include consultation, analysis, or input from resource agencies that may be necessary to ensure compliance with other applicable environmental law.

SAFETEA included several provisions that applied to projects that require an EIS. Section 6002 amended Title 23 by adding "Efficient Environmental Reviews for Project Decision-making" (§138). It established a new environmental review process applicable to all highways, transit, and multi-modal projects requiring an EIS. Among other requirements, the new process

- requires the project sponsor to notify DOT of the type of work, termini, length, general location of the proposed project, and a statement of any anticipated federal approvals;
- establishes a new entity required to participate in the NEPA process, referred to as a "participating agency," which includes any federal, state, tribal, regional, and local government agencies that *may have an interest in* the project;[33]
- requires the lead agency to establish a plan for coordinating public and agency participation in and comment on the environmental review process for a project or category of projects;
- requires the lead agency to establish a 60-day deadline on agency and public comments on a draft EIS and a 30-day deadline on all other comment periods in the environmental review process, except under certain circumstances (e.g., the deadline is extended by the lead agency for "good cause"); and
- prohibits claims seeking judicial review of a permit, license, or approval issued by a federal agency for highway or transit projects unless they are filed within 180 days after publication of a notice in the *Federal Register* announcing the final agency action, unless a shorter time is specified in the federal law under which the judicial review is allowed (previously, the six-year limit under the Administrative Procedure Act applied to NEPA-related claims).

DOT has produced guidance to help state DOTs implement SAFETEA's revised environmental review process and modified regulations implementing NEPA to reflect SAFETEA's amendments to Title 23.[34]

Table 3. Required Elements of an EIS as Implemented by FHWA

Elements of an EIS	Definition/Description
Purpose and need statement (§1502.13)	A brief statement, developed by the lead agency, specifying the underlying purpose of a project and the need to which the agency is responding. According to FHWA, this section may be the most important, as it establishes why the agency is proposing to spend large amounts of taxpayers' money while at the same time causing significant environmental impacts. A clear, well-justified statement explains to the public and decision makers that the use of funds is necessary and worthwhile, particularly as compared to other needed highway projects. The statement forms the basis on which potential alternatives to meet that need are identified and a final alternative is ultimately selected. It cannot be so narrow that it effectively defines competing "reasonable alternatives" out of consideration. The "purpose" may be a discussion of the goals and objective. The "need" may be a discussion of existing conditions that call for some improvement, including those applicable to transportation demand, safety, legislative direction, urban transportation plan consistency, modal interrelationships, system linkage, and the condition of an existing facility.
Alternatives (§1502.14)	Defined as the "heart" of the EIS, this section includes the identification and evaluation of all reasonable alternatives that may meet a project's purpose and need. FHWA requires the range of alternatives to include a discussion of how and why all reasonable alternatives were selected for consideration, and to explain why other alternatives were eliminated from detailed study. Each alternative, and its associated impacts, must be evaluated in sufficient detail to allow decision makers and the public an opportunity to compare the merits of each option.
Affected environment (§1502.15)	A succinct description of the environment of the area(s) to be affected or created by the alternatives under consideration. DOT requires this section to include a description of the existing social, economic, and environmental setting of the area potentially affected by all alternatives presented in the EIS. Data may include demographics of the general population served by the proposed project, as well as an identification of socially, economically, and environmentally sensitive locations or features in the proposed project area. For example, the EIS should identify the presence of affected minority or ethnic groups, parks, hazardous material sites, historic sites, or wetlands, among other factors.

Elements of an EIS	Definition/Description
Environmental Consequences (§1502.16)	Analysis of impacts of each project alternative on the affected environment, including a discussion of the probable beneficial and adverse social, economic, and environmental effects of each alternative. Where applicable, this section must include a description of the measures proposed to mitigate adverse impacts and methods of compliance with applicable legal requirements. FHWA recommends this section be devoted largely to a scientific analysis of the direct and indirect environmental effects of the proposed action relative to each alternative. Potential environmental consequences identified by FHWA include land use, farmland, social, economic, air quality, noise, water quality, wetland, wildlife, floodplain, or construction impacts; the requirement to obtain any permits; impacts to wild and scenic rivers, coastal barriers, threatened or endangered species, historic and archeological preservation, or hazardous waste sites; and any irreversible and irretrievable commitment of resources. This section would likely require input from other federal, state, tribal, or local agencies with expertise on the environmental consequences under review.
List of preparers (§1502.17)	List of names and qualifications of individuals responsible for preparing the EIS. FHWA requires this section to include lists of state and local agency personnel, including consultants, who were primarily responsible for preparing the EIS/performing environmental studies and FHWA personnel responsible for EIS preparation/review.
Appendix (§1502.18)	Prepared if necessary. An appendix normally consists of material that substantiates analysis fundamental to the impact statement.

Source: Congressional Research Service, taken from CEQ regulatory definitions under 40 C.F.R. §1502 and requirements and definitions applicable to highway projects included in FHWA guidance "NEPA and Transportation Decisionmaking: The Importance of Purpose and Need in Environmental Documents," and "Guidance for Preparing and Processing Environmental and Section 4(f) Documents."

The National Cooperative Highway Research Program conducted a survey of state DOTs to determine their impressions of the new environmental review process established by SAFETEA. The DOTs responding to the survey were generally favorable regarding the act's requirements.[35] In particular, there was wide approval of the 180-day statute of limitations.[36] However, survey respondents expressed concerns about some provisions, including their impressions that it represented no major change from what state DOTs were doing previously; it duplicated existing coordination procedures; and DOT already involved outside agencies prior to implementing the new procedures.

Further, many survey respondents expressed concern that some requirements of the new environmental review process seemed to run counter to streamlining initiatives by creating additional requirements that could have a negative impact on schedules and budgets.[37]

Under Section 6005, SAFETEA amended Title 23 to establish a "Surface Transportation Project Delivery Pilot Program" (§327). The pilot program allowed Oklahoma, California, Texas, Ohio, and Alaska to assume certain federal environmental review responsibilities (in addition to the assumption of CE determinations established under Section 6004, discussed above). Responsibility could be assumed for environmental reviews required under NEPA, or any federal law, for one or more highway projects within the state. As a condition of assuming federal authority, Congress required the state to waive its right to sovereign immunity against actions brought by citizens in federal court and consent to the jurisdiction of federal courts. That is, the state would become solely liable for complying with and carrying out the federal authority that it consents to assume.

To date, only California has agreed to and developed a program to participate in the pilot program. Other states declined, primarily due to state legislature concerns regarding the potential liability associated with assuming federal responsibility for NEPA.

Additionally, some state transportation agency officials and stakeholders with an interest in transportation project development have expressed concern over DOT requirements implementing the pilot program (as required pursuant to the directive in Section 6005). Those objections have centered largely around DOT's requirement applicable to rights-of-way (ROW) acquisitions in states that choose to assume federal authority under NEPA. As discussed earlier, one of NEPA's primary aims is to ensure that federal agencies consider the impacts of their actions before proceeding with them. The NEPA process cannot simply document a decision that has already been made. This requirement means that federal funds cannot be used for ROW acquisitions (an action that could indicate that a final project decision has been made) before the NEPA process is complete. Currently, states may make ROW acquisitions using state funds on an at-risk basis. That is, they may purchase land using state funds, but risk losing future federal funding for that purchase if the project ultimately involves an alternative that does not use that property. By assuming DOT's authority, a state would assume federal agency-level responsibility to comply with NEPA. DOT has found that would mean, in its capacity as a federal agency, the state would be precluded from making such advanced ROW acquisitions.

Some have argued that the loss of a state's ability to make at-risk ROW acquisitions has been a disincentive to states that may otherwise want to assume federal authority under NEPA. However, when the fear of taking on federal liability and subjecting the state to the jurisdiction of federal court were primary reasons that states did not want to assume NEPA authority, it is unclear how states could be protected from potential judicial review if they are allowed to complete a transaction that *could appear* to violate one of NEPA's primary goals. Although state DOTs may be willing to accept that risk, a state legislature may not, particularly when an incentive for a state to assume the federal role under NEPA is to eliminate FHWA's oversight of the NEPA process (e.g., FHWA's legal sufficiency review of an EIS).

Environmental Assessments (EAs)

The third category of NEPA document is an EA. It is required for an action that is not a CE and does not clearly require an EIS, or where FHWA believes an EA would assist in determining the need for an EIS. An EA is intended to be a concise public document that serves to provide sufficient evidence and analysis for determining whether to prepare an EIS or a Finding of No Significant Impact (FONSI).[38]

In preparing an EA, the applicant, in consultation with FHWA, is required to consult with interested agencies at the earliest appropriate time to determine the project scope; determine which aspects of the proposed action have potential for social, economic, or environmental impact; identify alternatives and measures which might mitigate adverse environmental impacts; and identify other environmental review and consultation requirements which should be performed concurrently with the EA.[39]

The EA is subject to FHWA approval before it is made available to the public. The document itself need not be circulated, but must be made available for public inspection and comment (typically for at least 30 days). A notice of availability must be sent to state- and area-wide clearinghouses and should be published locally. Depending on FHWA-approved state procedures, a public hearing may or may not be required.

FHWA requires the basis of a request for a FONSI be clearly and adequately documented. Like an EIS, the EA or FONSI is required to clearly document compliance with NEPA and all other applicable environmental laws, executive orders, and related requirements. An approved FONSI functions as the final agency decision on a project.

Like projects processed as CEs, determining the time it takes to complete an EA is difficult. Local and state transportation officials do not routinely, nor could they easily, track the time it takes to complete an EA. A distinct end point could be identified (issuance of a FONSI), but a starting point may be hard to identify. Further, since EAs likely require limited environmental review or analysis under NEPA, any analysis or review that is prepared to support a FONSI would likely be required under separate state or federal law. However, transportation agency officials have complained that EAs sometimes approach the length of an EIS. If that is the case, factors indirectly related to the NEPA compliance likely apply to the project. For example, a project that may involve local controversy or opposition, but still have no significant impacts, may require more analysis or documentation than anticipated. Also, a project with substantial environmental impacts to certain resources may require time-consuming consultation, analysis, or approvals from agencies outside DOT to confirm that no significant impacts will occur, or it could be an indication that an EIS should have been prepared initially.

Agency Roles and Responsibilities in the NEPA Process

The NEPA document is prepared by a "lead agency," and may require input and analysis from "cooperating" or "participating" agencies. Depending on the environmental impacts of a given project, both the lead and cooperating agencies are obligated to meet certain federal requirements. The time it takes to meet those obligations has been identified by transportation agencies as a potential source of frustration or project delay.

Lead Agencies

The "lead agency" is the federal agency responsible for preparing the NEPA document.[40] DOT must serve as the lead federal agency for a federally funded transportation project (FHWA generally serves as the lead for highway projects). The direct recipient of federal funds for the project must serve as a joint lead agency (a requirement explicitly established under SAFETEA). For a federal-aid highway project, that is typically the state DOT, but may include a local agency project sponsor or a federally recognized Indian tribal governmental unit. At the discretion of the required lead agencies, other federal, state, or local governmental entities may act as joint lead agencies. These include, but are not limited to toll, port, and turnpike authorities and metropolitan planning organizations (MPOs). For example, the U.S. Department of Homeland Security may serve as a joint lead agency with DOT and the project sponsor on a transportation improvement at a national border crossing.

In practice, the entity seeking federal funds will prepare the NEPA document, and other supporting environmental review documents, with guidance from FHWA (as necessary or as requested). FHWA, however, has ultimate responsibility to ensure that a project seeking federal funds will comply with the various laws, regulations, and executive orders applicable to the project. In that capacity, before final approval and project funding, FHWA is required to independently evaluate the necessary environmental documents and review the legal sufficiency of a final EIS[41] or Section 4(f) evaluation.[42] This review is intended to ensure that the Section 4(f) evaluation or NEPA document is consistent with legal requirements. It includes a review of the documentation and associated compliance efforts to determine if those efforts are sufficient to assure compliance with applicable law. A separate technical review of the final NEPA/Section4(f) document is also conducted by FHWA, prior to document approval.

Cooperating and, after SAFETEA, Participating Agencies

The lead agency must consult with and obtain the comments of any federal agency that has "jurisdiction by law or special expertise with respect to any environmental impact involved" in an action that requires an EIS.[43] In CEQ's NEPA regulations, those agencies are identified as "cooperating" agencies.[44] Pursuant to directive from Congress in SAFETEA, DOT's NEPA regulations were supplemented to also identify "participating" agencies, which may include any federal and non-federal agencies that may have an interest in the project.[45]

At the request of the lead agency, the cooperating agency is required to assume responsibility for developing information and preparing environmental analyses, including portions of the EIS related to its special expertise. Cooperating agencies are also obligated to provide comments on the NEPA document on areas within their jurisdiction, expertise, or authority. For projects requiring an EIS, that role may be set out in a memorandum of understanding or agreement between the agencies. The lead agency is also required to request comments from appropriate state, local, or tribal agencies; any agency that has requested to receive EISs on similar actions; and the project applicant.[46]

CEQ regulations specify requirements for inviting and responding to comments on the draft EIS (including requirements that specify a cooperating agency's duty to comment on the draft).[47] The lead agency is required to consider those comments and respond in one of the following ways:

- modify proposed alternatives, including the proposed action;
- develop and evaluate alternatives not previously considered;

- supplement, improve, or modify its analyses;
- make factual corrections in the EIS; or
- explain why the comments do not warrant further response from the lead agency, citing the sources, authorities, or reasons that support its position.[48]

As illustrated in the choices listed above, the lead agency is not precluded from moving forward with a project if it explains why a cooperating agency's comments do not warrant further response. However, FHWA suggests that every reasonable effort be made to resolve interagency disagreements on actions before processing the final EIS. If significant issues remain unresolved, the final EIS shall identify those issues and any consultation or other effort made to resolve them.

Some highway projects have involved disagreements regarding the appropriate authority and extent of involvement of coordinating agencies in the NEPA process. For example, in 2003, Transportation Secretary Norman Mineta requested CEQ Chairman James Connaughton to clarify the role of lead and cooperating agencies in developing EIS statements of project purpose and need statements.[49] Secretary Mineta cited the sometimes lengthy interagency debates over those statements as a cause of delay in highway project development. In his response, Chairman Connaughton referred to CEQ regulations specifying that the lead agency has the authority and responsibility to define a project's purpose and need. Further, Chairman Connaughton referenced previous federal court decisions giving deference to the lead agency in determining a project's purpose and need. Chairman Connaughton's letter also quotes CEQ's regulations, citing the lead agency's "responsibilities throughout the NEPA process for the 'scope, objectivity, and content of the entire statement or of any other responsibility' under NEPA."

Public Involvement

To meet NEPA's goal applicable to public participation in federal decision making, CEQ's regulations require agencies to provide public notice of NEPA-related hearings, public meetings, and the availability of environmental documents so as to inform public stakeholders.[50] DOT procedures extend beyond those established under CEQ regulations to reflect requirements applicable to "public hearings" established under Title 23.[51] For example, EAs do not need to be circulated, but must be made available to the public through notices of availability in local, state, or regional clearinghouses, newspapers, and other means. Depending on a state's public involvement procedures (approved by FHWA), a public hearing may or may not be required for projects that proceed with an EA. Pursuant to DOT regulations implementing NEPA, documentation necessary to demonstrate compliance with Title 23's public hearing requirements (e.g., public comments or hearing transcripts) must be included in the final EIS or FONSI, as applicable.

Stakeholders that comment on surface transportation projects may be expected to vary depending on a project's impacts. They may include individuals or groups who may benefit from or be adversely impacted by the project, or special interest groups with concerns about the project's impacts on certain affected environments. For example, a highway project that involves upgrading existing roadways may involve construction activities that would affect adjacent homes or businesses. The project may elicit comments from the local business community (e.g., individual businesses, the Chamber of Commerce, or local development organizations) or area homeowners. A project that may affect sensitive environmental resources, such as wetlands or endangered species, may generate comments from local or national environmental organizations. If a member of the public has concerns about a project's impacts, comments may be directed at virtually any element of the NEPA process or related documentation. Someone may disagree with the definition of project's purpose and need discussion, the range of "reasonable" alternatives selected for consideration and analysis, or the identified level of significance of the project's impacts (e.g., a FONSI was issued when the individual felt an EIS should have been required). Issues that arise during the public comment period may also be the subject of legal action. Critics of NEPA charge that those who disapprove of a federal project will use NEPA as the basis for litigation to delay or halt that project. Others argue that litigation results only when agencies do not comply with NEPA.[52]

Actual litigation played a prominent role in NEPA's early implementation. However, it may be the *threat* of litigation that affects its current implementation. The number of NEPA-related lawsuits filed annually against FHWA is low.[53] Still, the potential threat of litigation may result in an effort to prepare a "litigation-proof" NEPA document. This may be the case particularly for projects that are costly, technically complex (potentially requiring compliance with multiple environmental laws), or controversial (e.g., opposed by or individuals affected by the project or groups that anticipate adverse impacts to resources of concern to them). Some look at this positively, asserting that the fear of a lawsuit makes agencies more likely to adhere to NEPA's requirements. Others counter that the threat of litigation may lead to the generation of wasteful documentation and analyses that do not add value to, and slow, decision making.

Demonstrating Compliance with Additional Requirements

Unlike NEPA, which will apply in some way to all federally funded highway projects, additional environmental requirements applicable to a project will depend on site-specific conditions and potential impacts to resources at the site. For example, what and how requirements may apply to a project will depend on its effect on water quality, water resources, and land use as well as community, visual, noise, or social impacts, to name a few. While a wide array of requirements may apply to federally funded highway projects, certain federal requirements apply more commonly than other requirements. Also, certain compliance requirements have been identified by transportation stakeholders as those more likely to delay the environmental review process (see surveys and studies listed in **Appendix**). The most commonly applicable laws, and selected compliance requirements, are listed in **Table 4**. As illustrated by the requirements listed in **Table 4**, when a federal highway project involves regulated impacts to certain resources, an agency with jurisdiction over that resource may be required to provide some level of analysis, consultation, or approval before a project can proceed. Resulting consultation or approval may include directive(s) to the project sponsor regarding how or whether the proposed project may use the resource. These requirements can lengthen the time it takes to complete the overall environmental review process, if outside agency opinions, input, and/or evaluations are required before the NEPA review can be completed. Whether such requirements will lead to project delays could depend on a host of factors such as whether the project sponsor anticipated the need for outside agency approval or the workload of the agency processing the approval.

To integrate the NEPA compliance process and avoid duplication of effort associated with a project's overall environmental compliance obligations, CEQ's NEPA regulations specify that, to the fullest extent possible, agencies must prepare the NEPA documentation concurrently with any other environmental requirements. The appropriate NEPA documentation should demonstrate compliance with all applicable environmental requirements. It must indicate any federal permits, licenses, and other approvals required to implement the proposed project. This means that compliance requirements of any additional environmental laws, regulations, or executive orders must be identified (but not necessarily completed) during the NEPA process. If full compliance is not possible by the time the final NEPA document is prepared, the document should reflect consultation with the appropriate agencies and provide reasonable assurance that the requirements will be met.

**Table 4. Federal Law Commonly Applicable to
FHWA-Approved Projects**

Federal Law	Selected Compliance Requirements
Section 4(f)	For projects that would use a 4(f) resource, an evaluation or a determination of *de minimis* impacts must be prepared (see the discussion regarding "Preservation of parklands" in the "Requirements Applicable to Federal-aid Highways" section). The evaluation or *de minimis* impacts determination requires some level of consultation with or concurrence from the official with jurisdiction over the resource (e.g., the Department of the Interior's U.S. Fish and Wildlife Service (FWS); federal, state or local park authorities; or the designated SHPO).
Section 106 of the National Historic Preservation Act	For projects that may affect a site included, or eligible for inclusion, in the National Register of Historic Places, FHWA must consult with the Advisory Council on Historic Preservation (ACHP) or the designated SHPO to determine impacts to the site and seek ways to avoid, minimize, or mitigate adverse impacts. Affected parties must be involved in mitigation plans.
Endangered Species Act (Section 7)	FHWA must prepare a biological assessment when the presence of threatened or endangered animals or plants is suspected to occur in the vicinity of a project. FHWA must consult with the federal agency of jurisdiction (FWS or the Department of Commerce's National Marine Fisheries Service (NMFS)) that will issue a biological opinion on whether the proposed action would jeopardize the continued existence of listed species, or destroy or adversely modify their designated critical habitats.
The Clean Water Act (Section 404)	Requires that the discharge of dredge and fill materials into navigable waters of the United States be done in accordance with review and permitting procedures administered by the Corps, under guidelines developed by EPA. Other federal agencies potentially involved in permit evaluation process include FWS or NMFS.

Source: Congressional Research Service, taken from requirements listed in FHWA's "Summary of Environmental Legislation Affecting Transportation," at http:// www.fhwa.dot.gov/environment/env_sum.htm.

Note: This is not intended to be an exhaustive list of federal requirements potentially applicable to federally funded highway projects or a complete description of potentially applicable compliance requirements established pursuant to each law. However, the selected requirements illustrate the potential need to obtain permits or consult with agencies outside DOT. Further, federal laws selected for listing in this table represent those identified by transportation agency officials as a common source of delay in completing the environmental review process.

ENVIRONMENTAL REVIEWS
AND PROJECT DEVELOPMENT

To understand how the environmental review process may affect project delivery, it is useful to understand how the process fits into overall project development, as well as the challenges associated with measuring each stage of that development. It is also useful to recognize root causes of delay in completing the environmental review process, as well as how the process can lead to more efficient project development.

Stages of Project Development

Federal-aid highway funds are generally apportioned to each state by FHWA for the construction, reconstruction, and improvement of highways and bridges on eligible highway routes, and for other special-purpose programs. Individual state DOTs are responsible for determining how and on which projects those funds will be spent. In making that determination, multiple activities and decisions occur from the time a tribal or state DOT, metropolitan planning organization, or local program agency (such as a municipal public works agency) identifies a transportation-related need and a project addressing that need is constructed.

Each stage of project development is initiated and completed largely at the local, tribal, or state level, with ultimate project approval at the federal level—from FHWA for federally funded highway projects. Although the names and details of each step may vary from state to state, they generally include project planning, preliminary design and environmental review, final design and right-of-way acquisition, and project construction. Activities common to each phase of the project development process, including maintenance activities that may take place after project construction, are described in **Table 5**. The table also identifies potential environmental compliance obligations that may occur in each stage of project development.

Frequently, "environmental review" is considered synonymous with "NEPA compliance." That is not the case. However, completion of the NEPA compliance process and the overall environmental review process are linked by DOT's requirement that a project cannot be approved and subsequent stages of project development cannot proceed until the project sponsor appropriately documents compliance with NEPA and other applicable environmental requirements.

Table 5. Stages of Federal-Aid Highway Project Development

Common Project Activities and Environmental Compliance Obligations in Each Phase of Development		
Project Phase	**Description/Common Activities**	**Common Environmental Compliance Obligations**
Planning	Transportation program or project planning involves a cooperative process designed to foster involvement by all users of the planned system—such as the business community, community groups, environmental organizations, the traveling public, freight operators, and the general public. During this stage, a proactive public participation process is conducted by the metropolitan planning organization (MPO), state DOT, and transit operators. Among other activities, MPOs and state DOTs identify current and projected future transportation problems and needs, and analyze, through detailed planning studies, various transportation improvement strategies to address those needs. They also develop long-range plans and short-range programs for alternative capital improvement and operational strategies for moving people and goods.	Efforts have been made, in both FHWA guidance and statutory directive from Congress, to link statewide and metropolitan planning to the environmental review process. For example, Section 6001of SAFETEA requires the development of long-range transportation plans to include consultations with resource agencies responsible for land-use management, natural resources, environmental protection, conservation, and historic preservation, which may involve comparisons of resource maps and inventories; discussion of potential mitigation activities; and participation plans that identify a process for stakeholder involvement.
Preliminary design and environmental review	A project applicant identifies the preliminary engineering issues, such as proposed alignment of roadways, costs, and project details. This stage includes preliminary engineering and other activities and analyses, such as topographic or metes and bounds surveys, geotechnical investigations, hydrologic or hydraulic analysis, utility engineering, traffic studies, financial plans, revenue estimates, hazardous materials assessments, and general estimates of the types and quantities of materials and other work needed to establish parameters for the final design.	An applicant for federal-aid funds must determine the appropriate NEPA document to be prepared and identify various resources potentially affected by a proposed project and its alternatives. The final NEPA document must identify and demonstrate compliance with any other applicable environmental requirement, to the maximum extent possible, including completing necessary environmental or engineering studies, outside agency coordination or approvals, and public involvement.

Table 5. (Continued)

Common Project Activities and Environmental Compliance Obligations in Each Phase of Development		
Project Phase	**Description/Common Activities**	**Common Environmental Compliance Obligations**
Final design and right-of-way acquisition	Final construction plans and detailed construction specifications for the selected project alternative are prepared. If necessary, property appraisals and the acquisition of rights-of-way (ROW) or property to mitigate environmental impacts are made. Property acquisition that may involve the relocation of residents and businesses must be done in accordance with the Uniform Act of 1970. Also, if necessary, utilities are relocated. Project costs are finalized.	Property or material purchases cannot proceed until the NEPA document is approved by FHWA. Property acquisitions must be completed in compliance with requirements identified in the document. If late changes to the project are required, the environmental review process may have to be revisited if design changes result in unanticipated or previously unidentified environmental impacts.
Construction	The state DOT, or other project sponsor, requests and evaluates bids, and awards contracts. Project construction must reflect decisions made during the planning, environmental review, and design stages of project development.	Necessary permits or other compliance requirements identified during environmental review must be in place. Mitigation measures must be complete (e.g., installation of noise barriers or implementation of wetland mitigation). If elements of the project change, the environmental review process may have to be revisited if changes result in unanticipated environmental impacts.
Maintenance	Although not considered part of project development, the majority of projects funded under FHWA-approved programs involve activities that may be broadly described as "maintenance." Highway maintenance may include modernization through roadway resurfacing, restoration, rehabilitation, reconstruction, or adding shoulders or auxiliary lanes. Bridge maintenance may include rehabilitation, reconstruction, or replacement.	Identifying, planning, and implementing necessary maintenance activities are likely initiated and carried out at the local level, with state DOT approval. Maintenance activities would commonly involve a CE determination as well as an assessment of impacts that may require compliance with additional environmental requirements (e.g., impacts to historic sites or structures or endangered species habitat).

Source: Congressional Research Service, based on a review of state DOT practices.

Challenges in Measuring Stages of Project Development

There are distinct activities associated with each stage of project development. However, the following factors make it difficult to estimate the time it takes to complete each stage:

- Most state and local transportation agencies do not maintain a centralized source of data tracking the time it takes to complete transportation projects. Further, there is no acceptable measure of when a project is delivered in a timely manner versus delayed. A project or a stage of its development may be considered "delayed" if it took the project sponsor longer than anticipated.
- Most state and local transportation agencies do not attempt to extract and measure the time it takes to complete individual activities attributable to a single stage of development (e.g., activities categorized distinctly as applicable to "environmental review"). Further, tracking that data may be difficult since elements of one phase may overlap with another (e.g., project planning activities may include elements of environmental review) and a distinct start and end point of individual activities may be difficult to identify.
- Project development may start, stop, and restart for reasons unrelated to environmental compliance. For example, EIS preparation may begin with publication of a NOI, but preparation may stop and restart due to changes in state priorities, funding availability, or a host of other issues unrelated to NEPA. In such cases, the time between issuing a NOI and ROD are an inaccurate measure of the NEPA process.
- Differences between state DOT project development processes make it difficult to establish a nationally applicable measure of project development stages. Also, the influence of tribal- or state-specific environmental compliance requirements makes it difficult to isolate the time it takes to comply with federal requirements.

Considering these points, it is difficult to determine either the time it takes to meet specific elements of the environmental review process (e.g., NEPA compliance or agency consultations under the Endangered Species Act) or the degree to which completing the process delays project delivery. Further, it is not possible to assert, with any degree of accuracy, broad, nationally applicable values to the time it takes to complete the environmental review process. For example, there are no data available to substantiate a statement such as "environmental compliance accounts for X% to Y% of surface transportation project development time," or "compliance with NEPA or Clean Water Act permitting requirements delays X% to Y% of projects for X to Y months/years." Instead, it may be possible to determine "bridge reconstruction or rehabilitation in state A takes from X to Y months/years" if state A is one that tracks such information.

Also, it may be generally stated that the time it takes to deliver larger, more complex or controversial projects takes longer to complete than is typical for the majority of FHWA-approved highway projects (e.g., maintenance and rehabilitation projects). In addition to taking longer to complete due to their potential cost, size, and complexity, they will likely require compliance with more state, tribal, and federal requirements and may generate more public interest or opposition.

In 2002, the General Accounting Office (GAO) released a report that attempted to determine the typical amount of time it takes to complete overall project delivery as well as individual phases of project development for certain federally funded highway projects.[54] Data for this report were compiled based on the professional judgment of FHWA staff, staff of state departments of transportation, and transportation associations. According to FHWA, planning, gaining approval for, and constructing federally funded major highway projects that involved new construction typically took from nine to 19 years from planning to construction. FHWA estimated that the preliminary design and environmental review phase for those projects typically took from one to five years, depending on the complexity of the design and possible environmental impacts that must be considered.[55] It was noted that projects studied in the GAO report included those that would typically require an EIS and represent a small percentage of federally funded projects. It was also noted that, while there are many reasons new highway construction projects may take a long time to complete, most studies on project delivery focused only on the timely resolution of environmental issues to improve project completion times, rather than examining all aspects of project development.[56]

Causes of Delay in Completing Environmental Reviews

Although the extent to which the environmental review process may delay project delivery is unclear, it is generally not disputed that the time it takes to demonstrate compliance with environmental requirements can be time-consuming, particularly in cases where EIS preparation is required. Also, while transportation agency officials may cite elements of the environmental review process as a source of frustration or delay, it is not clear what specific environmental compliance requirements currently and routinely lead to project delays or the root cause of those delays.[57] For example, a common complaint among transportation agency officials is that outside agencies (including FHWA review and approval of the final NEPA documents) do not provide necessary input or approval in a timely way. However, there is little information available that clearly indicates *why* that may be the case on anything other than a project-specific level.

Few studies have looked at the root causes of project delay directly attributable to the environmental review process. Available studies have looked at a limited number of major new construction projects that required an EIS. By their nature, those projects involve unique project-specific issues and are likely to involve complex design, engineering, and compliance issues. Causes of delay for those projects more likely represent the exception and not the rule.

A 2003 FHWA study that attempted to identify causes of delay in completing EISs was unable to identify common factors or conditions that directly or indirectly affected the time it took to complete the NEPA process.[58] Although timing varied by broad geographic region, it did not seem to vary in relation to the majority of other variables considered (e.g., the presence of certain "controversial issues" or the required participation of agencies outside DOT). Instead, it was observed that the time it took to complete the NEPA process may have been more affected by external social and economic factors associated with broad geographic regions of the country.[59]

Subsequent, albeit limited, study data and anecdotal evidence regarding individual projects also point to factors external to environmental reviews as those most likely to delay the process. In particular, causes of delay in completing environmental reviews arise primarily from potentially overlapping local and project-specific issues including, but not limited to, the following:

- **Local issues**—the project's level of priority among others proposed in the state; changes in funding availability; concerns of local property owners; or opposition to the project (which may or may not be connected to environmental issues).
- **Project-specific issues**—the project's technical complexity; changes in project scope or design; lawsuits or the threat of litigation (which

may or may not be connected to environmental issues); poor consultant work; issues with city documentation; issues with new alignment or coordination with other transportation projects; or land use planning issues.[60]

As discussed previously, environmental requirements identified as a source of delay have been associated with selected requirements established under Section 4(f); the Endangered Species Act; the National Historic Preservation Act; and the Clean Water Act. If a project is delayed by requirements under those laws, that delay may be attributable to project-specific issues.

Efforts to identify specific problems or causes of delay in meeting requirements other than NEPA have found differing perceptions among resource agency and transportation agency officials. For example, in completing its obligations as part of the environmental review process, resource agencies have identified poor communication, problems with the project's alternative analysis, being given incorrect or incomplete information, disagreements or differences of opinion among agencies, or environmental or biological issues associated with the project. Transportation agency officials also cited disagreements or differences of opinion and environmental or biological issues associated with the project, but identified a lack of timely response from resource agencies as the primary problem.[61]

Benefits to the Environmental Review Process

When there is debate over potential options to expedite the environmental review process, that process may be viewed as simply an obstacle to overcome before a highway or bridge project can be built. Benefits to the process may be overlooked or hard to quantify. Potential benefits may generally be thought of as those associated with balancing transportation and infrastructure needs with environmental protection and community concerns. However, one benefit that is not often considered is the degree to which the environmental review process may ultimately save time and reduce overall project costs by identifying and avoiding problems in later stages of project development. A study prepared for the Transportation Research Board made this point when evaluating causes of delay in the construction phases of development.[62]

Among other findings, the study found that certain recognized management principles, identified as relevant to timely completion of highway construction projects, should be applied by state highway administrators and contractors. It found that adherence to these principles was often inconsistent and lacking, usually resulting in construction delays. Among the principles identified was the "Cost-Time Relationship," under which, the study found,

> More time spent in design identifying problems will reduce construction time and result in a shorter overall project time. A widely recognized principle is that spending more monies during planning and design will reduce the time and cost required for construction by avoiding unforeseen conditions, reducing to a minimum design errors and omissions, and developing schemes that will support the most efficient approach to construction. In the design phase, the opportunity to make decisions to influence the final project cost is greatest. Yet, the expenditure of project funds is comparatively minimal, typically about 10% of the capital budget.[63]

These study findings illustrate the potential problem with considering time spent in the planning or preliminary design stage as a delay. It is impossible to determine whether or how much time may be saved, and project delivery ultimately accelerated, by avoiding conditions identified early in the process.

EXPEDITING ENVIRONMENTAL REVIEWS

Lessons Learned

The potential for the environmental review process to expedite project delivery is illustrated in findings of a 2009 peer exchange between representatives from state DOTs and FHWA Division Offices. The exchange was intended to identify strategies to more effectively move complex environmental documents through the EIS process.[64] Participants presented information on projects in their states that had moved through the environmental review process quickly. They highlighted the challenges encountered, methods used to successfully and efficiently navigate the EIS process, and lessons learned from their experience. It was observed that the practices described by state DOTs represented a fundamental shift in the way agencies have conducted environmental reviews over the last 10 to 15 years. Those state DOTs were found to have

> embraced innovative and creative solutions to balance transportation and infrastructure needs with environmental protection and community concerns.

The environmental review processes for the successful projects ... were conducted in a collaborative and transparent manner, whereby [state DOTs] sought to include stakeholders early and often throughout development of the EIS. Such methods not only lead to a faster completion of the environmental review process, but perhaps more importantly, they result in the delivery of better quality projects, ones that fulfill the transportation needs of communities while maintaining protection of environmental resources at the same time.[65]

One recent event serves as a good example of how environmental compliance requirements can be coordinated efficiently. That event was the reconstruction of the I-35 bridge in Minneapolis after its August 1, 2007, collapse. A new bridge opened just over a year later on September 18, 2008. The timing of that bridge reconstruction led to the question "Why can't all projects be completed that quickly?"

The answer to this question can be found, in part, in an FHWA study that examined how the key elements of the environmental review process were completed after a bridge collapse.[66] A primary factor cited in the study was that, in the wake of an emergency, the major causes of surface transportation project delay are absent. The "major causes of delay" identified were a lack of funding or priority in the state for the project; local controversy; interested stakeholder or local opposition; or insufficient political support.[67] Other potential causes of delay could still apply to emergency projects, including issues with the projects' complexity, poor consultant work, or the environmental review process.

The FHWA study looked at the Minnesota bridge collapse as well as other projects that involved bridge reconstruction after a collapse. Projects in the study illustrated how efficiently the environmental review process *could be* implemented if the more common sources of delay are absent and environmental review involves efficient interagency cooperation.

Bridge reconstruction for the I-35 project required the same environmental permits that would apply to any bridge reconstruction project of similar scope and scale. Despite the urgency of the project, there was no waiver or exemption from the environmental review or permit requirements. The replacement bridge was widened to accommodate future transit options, but did not increase capacity. The project fit the criteria necessary to be processed as a CE, but still required

- a permit issued by the Corps under Section 404 of the Clean Water Act;

- a bridge construction permit issued by the U.S. Coast Guard;
- an assessment of potential impacts to threatened and endangered species by a consultation team formed by FHWA, Minnesota DOT (MnDOT), and the Department of the Interior's U.S. Fish and Wildlife Service (FWS);
- a Minnesota Pollution Control Agency permit certifying compliance with the Clean Water Act's National Pollutant Discharge Elimination System and other requirements; and
- an assessment of potential cultural and historic issues through MnDOT's Cultural Resources Unit (CRU), in part, in accordance with a programmatic agreement with the Minnesota SHPO and tribes interested in reviewing state projects.

Efficient interagency coordination on the project was a factor identified as one associated with expedited reconstruction of the bridge. However, the efficiency of that agency interaction did not begin with this project. FHWA observed that staff from state and federal agencies involved in the environmental review process had worked collaboratively on past projects. The agencies established lines of communication and understood the tasks and concerns of each other's agencies. Those existing relationships led to a quick response among those agencies after the bridge collapse. Further, FHWA and MnDOT recognized that by limiting the scope of the project, the environmental review process was expedited because no expanded environmental review was needed (e.g., it met the criteria applicable to a CE). Further, federal and state resources were focused on this project—its completion was a priority to the state.

Apart from issues cited in the FHWA bridge study, MnDOT cited its use of a design-build procurement process as an important factor in the expediting project completion. A "design-build" process brings designers and contractors together early in the project development process and allows for a shortened process completion time by overlapping design and construction.[68]

Lessons learned from projects completed relatively quickly as well as suggested solutions from transportation agency officials[69] involve certain common approaches or procedures that have or could streamline the environmental review process. Those approaches include the following:

- efficient interagency communication and project coordination;
- early and continued communication with stakeholders affected by a project;

- improvements in internal processes and procedures;
- demonstrated agency commitment to priority projects and project schedules; and/or
- programmatic approaches to meeting compliance obligations.

Each of these approaches can be implemented under existing standards and requirements applicable to federally funded highway projects. For example, CEQ and DOT regulations implementing NEPA include explicit requirements intended to identify potential environmental issues early in the project development process and coordinate efficient interagency cooperation. CEQ also provides federal agencies with guidance on improving the efficiency and timeliness of their environmental reviews under NEPA.[70] DOT provides guidance and information intended to assist state and local agencies in implementing the environmental review process more efficiently.[71]

Administrative Efforts

In 2009, DOT initiated its "Every Day Counts" program to identify and implement approaches to shortening project delivery (among other goals). The program includes an evaluation of potential changes in DOT's role in implementing the environmental review process, including the following efforts:

- **Improve the link between project planning and environmental review**—sets up a framework for incorporating planning documents and decisions from the earliest stages of project planning into the environmental review process.
- **Enhance legal sufficiency reviews**—uses the process to identify the most common problems in NEPA and Section 4(f) document development, their root causes, and the measures local and state transportation agencies can take to avoid the problems; and encourages reviews when documents are in their draft stage, reducing the potential need for multiple legal reviews of a "final" document and helping to resolve conflict and potential controversy earlier in the process, when project schedules can better accommodate the change.
- **Expand the use of programmatic agreements**—identify new and existing programmatic agreements that may be expanded to a regional or national level.

- **Encourage the use of existing regulatory flexibility**—clarify existing requirements applicable to activities that may be allowed during the preliminary design phase of development and to ROW acquisition and utility relocation.

These issues identified by both DOT and state transportation agencies illustrate the need to more efficiently implement existing requirements or to identify barriers to implementing them.

CONCLUSION

There is little debate that delays in transportation project delivery can result in higher project costs, as well as delay potential positive economic advantages such as bringing project-related jobs to the community. Also, it is known that completing the environmental review process takes time, sometimes years for complex, major projects. Meeting environmental compliance requirements may result in project delays or, at least, a project taking longer than anticipated by its sponsor. However, what is unclear is whether or what specific elements of the environmental review process routinely delay project delivery.

The time it takes to complete the NEPA process is often the focus of debate over project delays attributable to the environmental review process. However, the influence of environmental requirements established under Title 23 and other federal law call into question the degree to which changes in the NEPA process will expedite the environmental reviews and accelerate project delivery. Further, although there are no comprehensive data and available information tends to be anecdotal, when delays in the environmental review process have been identified, they primarily stemmed from local or project-specific issues (e.g., project complexity, changes in state priorities, or late changes in project scope).

Regardless of potential changes to the NEPA process or the overall environmental review process, local factors will strongly influence project delivery time. State or local decision makers will continue to have the most significant influence on project delivery in their capacity to establish (and change) project priorities, allocate available funds, and be influenced by local controversy or project opposition. A project's environmental review process may be efficiently executed and involve no delays in the process itself, but still take decades or never be completed if local and state issues are acting against the project.

The potential success of efforts intended to expedite the environmental review process would involve evidence that transportation projects were delivered more quickly. However, considering the limits to measuring the time it takes to complete the environmental review process, the relative success of a particular approach may be gauged in terms of the degree to which state or local transportation agencies find it useful in meeting their environmental compliance obligations.

Compared to transportation planning and project development during construction of the Interstate Highway System, state and local transportation agencies are more inclined to consider a project's effects on communities and resources. Apart from any potential changes to federal environmental review requirements, local and state agency decisions regarding transportation project planning, funding, and development will continue to be strongly influenced by a project's benefits and adverse effects to the environment and the community it serves.

APPENDIX. SURVEYS AND STUDIES APPLICABLE TO THE ENVIRONMENTAL REVIEW PROCESS

In this report, summary information and conclusions regarding factors applicable to measuring the stages of project development, the time it takes to complete the environmental review process, and primary sources of delay or perceptions among transportation agency officials regarding causes of delay in completing the environmental review process were drawn from data included in the following surveys and studies conducted by FHWA, GAO, universities, or transportation organizations:

Federal Highway Administration (available on FHWA's "Environmental Toolkit: Streamlining/Stewardship—Performance Reporting" website, http://environment.fhwa.dot.gov/strmlng/es10measures.asp).

- *Evaluating the Performance of Environmental Streamlining:* Phase II, an FHWA-commission study conducted by the Louis Berger Group, 2003.

- FHWA surveys, *Reasons for EIS Project Delays and Information on Timeliness on Completing the NEPA Process.*
- *Strategies and Approaches for Effectively Moving Complex Environmental Documents Through the EIS Process:* A Peer Exchange Report, prepared for FHWA by DOT's John A. Volpe National Transportation Systems Center Research and Innovative Technology Administration, January 2009.
- *FHWA/Gallup Study on Implementing Performance Measurement in Environmental Streamlining,* "Implementing Performance Measurement in Environmental Streamlining," May 2007.

Government Accountability Office.

- *Highway Infrastructure: Stakeholders' Views on Time to Conduct Environmental Reviews of Highway Projects,* GAO-03-534, May 23, 2003.
- *Highway Infrastructure: Preliminary Information on the Timely Completion of Highway Construction Projects,* GAO-02-1067T, September 19, 2002.

University and Transportation Organization Studies.

- *What Influences the Length of Time to Complete NEPA Reviews? An Examination of Highway Projects in Oregon and the Potential for Streamlining,* by Jennifer Dill, Center for Urban Studies, Nohad A. Toulan School of Urban Studies &Planning, Portland State University, submitted for presentation at the 85th Annual Meeting of the Transportation Research Board, November 15, 2005 (revised).
- *Causes and Extent of Environmental Delays in Transportation Projects,* prepared by TransTech Management, Inc., for the American Association of State Highway and Transportation Officials (AASHTO), December 2003.
- Environmental Streamlining: A Report on Delays Associated with the Categorical Exclusion and Environmental Assessment Processes, prepared by TransTech Management, Inc., for AASHTO, October 2000.

End Notes

[1] This report focuses on projects approved under programs administered by FHWA. Although they involve similar regulatory requirements, issues unique to transit projects approved under programs administered by the Federal Transit Administration (FTA) are not addressed in this report.

[2] Those requirements are largely established under Chapter 1, "Federal-aid Highways," of Title 23, "Highways" of the *U.S. Code*.

[3] In this report, reference to "federal-aid highways," "federal highways," or "federal highway projects" means projects that may receive federal funding pursuant to the Federal-aid Highways provisions of Title 23. Those projects include, but are not limited to, the initial construction, reconstruction, replacement, rehabilitation, restoration, or other improvements of a highway, road, street, parkway, right-of-way, bridge, or tunnel.

[4] See CRS Report R41947, *Accelerating Highway and Transit Project Delivery: Issues and Options for Congress*, by William J. Mallett and Linda Luther.

[5] The Safe, Accountable, Flexible, Efficient Transportation Equity Act: A Legacy for Users (SAFETEA-LU or SAFETEA; P.L. 109-59, for FY2005-FY2009) and the Transportation Equity Act for the 21st Century (TEA-21; P.L.105-178, for FY1998-FY2003).

[6] H.R. 7 was reported favorably by the House Transportation and Infrastructure Committee on February 13, 2012. MAP-21 passed the Senate on March 14, 2012.

[7] See *NEPA and Project Development: Program Overview* on FHWA's "Environmental Review Toolkit" webpage at http://environment.fhwa.dot.gov/projdev/index.asp.

[8] 23 C.F.R. Part 771.

[9] The National Highway System is approximately 160,000 miles of roadway important to the nation's economy, defense, and mobility.

[10] For more information about the Interstate Highway System, see the U.S. Department of Transportation's Federal Highway Administration website, "Celebrating the Eisenhower Interstate Highway System," http://www.fhwa.dot.gov/interstate/homepage.cfm.

[11] Report prepared by the John A. Volpe National Transportation Systems Center Research and Innovative Technology Administration, U.S. Department of Transportation for the Office of Project Development and Environmental Review, Federal Highway Administration, "Strategies and Approaches for Effectively Moving Complex Environmental Documents Through the EIS Process: A Peer Exchange Report," January 2009, available on the Federal Highway Administration's "Streamlining/Stewardship" website at http://environment.fhwa.dot.gov/strmlng/eisdocs.asp.

[12] For a discussion of issues related to freeway revolts and general issues with urban freeway construction, see "Paved with Good Intentions: Fiscal Politics, Freeways and the 20th Century American City," by Jeffrey A. Brown, Eric A. Morris, and Brian D. Taylor, in the University of California Transportation Center's *Access* magazine, Fall 2009, available at http://www.uctc.net/access/35/access35_Paved_with_Good_Intentions_Fiscal_Politics_.shtml.

[13] The term "Section 4(f)" refers to the section of the Department of Transportation Act of 1966 (P.L. 89-670) under which the requirement was originally set forth. It was initially codified at 49 U.S.C. §1653(f) and only applied to DOT agencies. Later that year, 23 U.S.C. §138 was added with somewhat different language, which applied only to the highway program. In 1983, as part of a general recodification of the DOT Act, §1653(f) was formally repealed and codified in 49 U.S.C. §303 with slightly different language. This provision no longer falls under a "Section 4(f)," but DOT has continued this reference, given that over the years, the whole body of provisions, policies, and case law has been collectively referenced as Section 4(f).

[14] Depending on project alternatives under consideration for a given project, compliance with Section 4(f) requirements can be complex. This report does not discuss those requirements

in detail. For more information, see the "Section 4(f)"website included in FHWA's "Environmental Review Toolkit," at http://www.environment.fhwa.dot.gov/4f/index.asp.

[15] *Citizens to Preserve Overton Park v. Volpe*, 401 U.S. 402 (1971).

[16] See Department of Transportation, "Parks, Recreation Areas, Wildlife and Waterfowl Refuges, and Historic Sites," final rule, 73 *Federal Register* 13367-13401, March 12, 2008.

[17] Air quality issues are also relevant to federal-aid highway project development. Under the Clean Air Act, FHWA must insure that transportation plans, programs, and projects conform to the state's air quality implementation plans. Conformance with a state implementation plan is largely determined during project planning. Issues associated with meeting federal air quality requirements are not discussed in this report.

[18] 40 C.F.R. §§1500-1508.

[19] 40 C.F.R. §1507.3.

[20] 23 C.F.R. Part 771.

[21] These statistics apply to projects funded under the Federal-aid Highway program. For more detail, see the Federal Highway Administration's "Highway Statistics for 2009: Obligation of Federal-Aid Highway Funds For Highway Improvements Fiscal Year 2009 (Intended to Show Only Projects Authorized in FY 2009)," Table FA-10, October 2010, available at http://www.fhwa.dot.gov/policyinformation/statistics/2009/fa10.cfm..

[22] That definition of "Major Projects" was included among provisions in Section 1904 of SAFETEA that amended the "Project approval and oversight" requirements under 23 U.S.C. §106. The identification of a project as "major," in this context, is unrelated to its potential distinction as a "major federal action significantly affecting the quality of the human environment" pursuant to NEPA under 42 U.S.C. §4332(c).

[23] See the *FHWA Active Project Status Report*, available on FHWA's "Project Delivery" website, https://fhwaapps.fhwa.dot.gov/foisp/publicActive.do.

[24] 23 C.F.R. §771.117(a); further DOT criteria used to determine whether a project would meet necessary CE criteria extend from CEQ regulations defining CEs at 40 C.F.R. §1508.4.

[25] 23 C.F.R. §771.117(b).

[26] Listed at 23 C.F.R. §771.117(c).

[27] Listed at 23 C.F.R. §771.117(d).

[28] 23 U.S.C. §326.

[29] For more information, see memorandum from the U.S. Department of Transportation, Federal Highway Administration, to Directors of Field Services and Division Administrators, regarding "Guidance on the State Assumption of Responsibility for Categorical Exclusions (CE)," April 6, 2006, available at http://www.fhwa.dot.gov/hep/6004memo.htm.

[30] 23 C.F.R. §771.115(a).

[31] 40 C.F.R. §1508.22.

[32] 40 C.F.R. §1502.9.

[33] This category of agency participant in the NEPA process differs from a "cooperating agency," discussed below, that is defined as an agency having jurisdiction by law or special expertise with respect to any environmental impact of a proposed project or project alternative.

[34] See "SAFETEA-LU Environmental Review Process, Final Guidance," November 15, 2006, available at http://www.fhwa.dot.gov/hep/section6002/index.htm and the Department of Transportation's "Environmental Impact and Related Procedures; Final Rule," 74 *Federal Register* 12517, March 24, 2009.

[35] See the National Cooperative Highway Research Program's "Legal Research Digest 54: Practice Under the Environmental Provisions of SAFETEA-LU," December 2010, available at http://onlinepubs.trb.org/onlinepubs/ nchrp/nchrp_lrd_54.pdf.

[36] There was also wide approval of changes made to Section 4(f) under SAFETEA Section 6002, applicable to *de minimis* project impacts (see "Requirements Applicable to Federal-aid Highways" regarding the "preservation of parklands" requirements).

[37] See the summary of survey respondent impressions of SAFETEA provisions at pp. 16-21.

[38] 40 C.F.R. §1508.9.

[39] 23 C.F.R. §771.119(b).

[40] See 40 C.F.R. §1508.16.

[41] 23 C.F.R. §771.125(b). A legal sufficiency review of an EA may be required if FHWA determines that details of the individual project warrant such a review.

[42] 23 C.F.R. §774.7(d).

[43] 42 U.S.C. §4332(2)(C).

[44] 40 C.F.R. §1508.5.

[45] Specific only to DOT's NEPA requirements, "participating" agencies for federal highway projects are defined at 23 C.F.R. §771.107(h) as a state, local, tribal, or federal agency that may have an interest in the proposed project and have accepted an invitation to participate in the environmental review process.

[46] 40 C.F.R. §1503.1.

[47] 40 C.F.R. §1503.

[48] 40 C.F.R. §1503.4.

[49] Text of Secretary Mineta's May 6, 2003, letter, and Chairman Connaughton's May 12, 2003, response, are available at http://www.environment.fhwa.dot.gov/guidebook/Ginterim.asp.

[50] 40 C.F.R. §§1500.2(d). 1506.6.

[51] 23 U.S.C. §128.

[52] Plaintiffs have generally cited some inadequacy in the NEPA documentation as the basis for filing NEPA-related lawsuits (see CEQ's *Litigation Surveys* for each year from 2001 to 2009 on its "NEPA Litigation" web page at http://ceq.hss.doe.gov/legal_corner/litigation. html). They may charge, among other things, that an EIS or EA did not include sufficient analysis of all project alternatives, did not consider all "reasonable" project alternatives, did not adequately analyze the effects of project alternatives, or that an EA was prepared when an EIS should have been (i.e., a FONSI was issued when impacts were in fact significant).

[53] From 2001 to 2009, NEPA-related lawsuits filed annually against FHWA ranged from a low of three to a high of 12; see CEQ's *Litigation Surveys* cited in footnote 52.

[54] U.S. General Accounting Office (now the Government Accountability Office), *Highway Infrastructure: Preliminary Information on the Timely Completion of Highway Construction Projects*, September 19, 2002.

[55] In addition to information from FHWA and state DOT staff, this report also looked at the time it took and the steps necessary to complete six new highway construction projects in California, Florida, and Texas (the largest in the state, in terms of federal funds received, and a randomly selected "medium-sized" project).

[56] Consistent with the factors that make it difficult to measure individual phases of project development, discussed above, GAO noted that federal and state governments do not maintain information centrally (or, in some cases, at all) on the time it takes to complete highway projects. GAO also noted that there was no accepted measuring stick with which to gauge whether project performance is "timely." To make its determination on project timing, GAO relied on a best estimate prepared by FHWA. According to FHWA, the estimate it provided to GAO was based on the professional judgment of its staff and several state DOTs.

[57] The identification of factors that currently affect project delivery is particularly relevant when considering legislative options to address potential causes of delay in the environmental review process. State DOTs have improved their environmental review procedures in the past 10 years. Also, FHWA has expanded its efforts to provide information and guidance on the process, including increased efforts to encourage states to implement programmatic agreements applicable to NEPA compliance and other environmental laws.

[58] Federal Highway Administration and the Louis Berger Group, *Evaluating the Performance of Environmental Streamlining: Phase II*, 2003, available on FHWA's "Streamlining/ Stewardship" website, http://www.environment.fhwa.dot.gov/strmlng/baseline/phase2rpt. asp.

[59] Ibid., under "Conclusions 4.2."

[60] Factors listed here are those that have been most commonly identified in surveys or studies conducted by FHWA and GAO, as well as selected university and transportation organizations. For a list of the surveys and studies used to prepare this report, see **Appendix**. Those surveys and studies have looked primarily at causes of delay applicable to projects that require an EIS.

[61] See "FHWA/Gallup Study on Implementing Performance Measurement in Environmental Streamlining," available at http://environment.fhwa.dot.gov/strmlng/gallup_05-07.asp.

[62] Thomas, H.R. and Ellis, R.D, *Avoiding Delays During the Construction Phase of Highway Projects*, Transportation Research Board, National Research Council, October 2001, NCHRP 20-24(12). Also see "The Root Causes of Delays in Highway Construction," a summary of the study's findings submitted for presentation by the authors at the TRB annual meeting in 2003, available at http://www.ltrc.lsu.edu/TRB_82/TRB2003-000646.pdf.

[63] "The Root Causes of Delays in Highway Construction," p. 3.

[64] *Strategies and Approaches for Effectively Moving Complex Environmental Documents Through the EIS Process: A Peer Exchange Report*, prepared by the John A. Volpe National Transportation Systems Center Research and Innovative Technology Administration, U.S. Department of Transportation for the Office of Project Development and Environmental Review, Federal Highway Administration, January 2009, available on FHWA's "Streamlining/Stewardship" website at http://environment.fhwa.dot.gov/strmlng/eisdocs.asp.

[65] Ibid., under "Recommendations for Successful Tools & Techniques."

[66] See "Meeting Environmental Requirements After a Bridge Collapse," prepared for the Office of Project Development and Environmental Review, Federal Highway Administration, U.S. Department of Transportation, and prepared by the John A. Volpe National Transportation Systems Center Research and Innovative Technology Administration, U.S. Department of Transportation, August 2008, available at http://www.environment.fhwa.dot.gov/projdev/bridge_casestudy.asp.

[67] Major sources of project delay cited in the bridge study are those identified in FHWA survey results included in **Appendix**.

[68] For more information about the bridge reconstruction project, see the Minnesota DOT "I-35W St. Anthony Falls Bridge" website at http://projects.dot.state.mn.us/35wbridge/index.html.

[69] See findings in the 2007 FHWA/Gallup study (cited in footnote 61).

[70] CEQ guidance "Improving the Process for Preparing Efficient and Timely Environmental Reviews under the National Environmental Policy Act," released on March 6, 2012, available at http://www.whitehouse.gov/administration/eop/ceq/initiatives/nepa/efficiencies-guidance. CEQ stated that the guidance is part of its broader effort to "modernize and reinvigorate" federal agency implementation of NEPA and to support goals established in President Obama's August 31, 2011, memorandum, "Speeding Infrastructure Development through More Efficient and Effective Permitting and Environmental Review." For information about CEQ pilot programs established to support those goals, see http://www.whitehouse.gov/administration/eop/ceq/initiatives/nepa/nepa-pilot-project.

[71] See FHWA's online "Environmental Review Toolkit," available at http://environment.fhwa.dot.gov/index.asp. It includes, for example, guidance and information regarding linking project planning and environmental requirements; NEPA requirements applicable to project development; a database of "lessons learned" related to streamlining and environmental stewardship; and guidance on compliance requirements such as those applicable to wetlands, Section 4(f), and historic preservation.

In: Federal Programs and Policies for Highways   ISBN: 978-1-62257-755-2
Editors: E.D. Campbell and E.Sanchez © 2013 Nova Science Publishers, Inc.

Chapter 4

EMERGENCY RELIEF PROGRAM: FEDERAL-AID HIGHWAY ASSISTANCE FOR DISASTER-DAMAGED ROADS AND BRIDGES[*]

Robert S. Kirk

SUMMARY

The major highways and bridges damaged during Hurricane Irene in 2011and the I-35W bridge collapse in Minneapolis of August 1, 2007 are part of the federal-aid highway system and were therefore eligible for assistance under the Federal Highway Administration's (FHWA's) Emergency Relief Program (ER). Following a natural disaster or catastrophic failure (such as the I-35W bridge), ER funds are made available for both emergency repairs and restoration of federal-aid highway facilities to pre-disaster conditions.

The ER program is administered through the state departments of transportation in close coordination with FHWA's division offices (there is one in each state). Although ER is a federal program, the decision to seek ER funding is made by the state, not by the federal government. Most observers see the close and ongoing relationship between the FHWA's staff at the state level and their state counterparts as facilitating a quick coordinated response to disasters.

---

[*] This is an edited, reformatted and augmented version of a Congressional Research Service publication, CRS Report for Congress R42021, from www.crs.gov, prepared for Members and Committees of Congress, dated September 23, 2011.

The program is funded by an annual $100 million authorization from the highway trust fund and general fund appropriations that are provided by Congress on a such sums as necessary basis. A number of issues have arisen in recent years:

- The scope of eligible activities funded by ER has grown via legislative or FHWA waivers of eligibility criteria or changes in definitions that have expanded the scope of ER projects, sometimes beyond repairing or restoring highways to pre-disaster condition.
- The $100 million annual authorization has been exceeded nearly every fiscal year, requiring appropriations that can lead to delay in funding permanent repairs.
- Congress has directed that in some cases ER fully fund projects, without the normal 10% or 20% state matching share, putting financial pressure on the federal side of disaster highway assistance.

State requests for ER funding are at times backlogged. In a deficit-reduction environment, it is questionable whether the ER program can continue to loosen eligibility restrictions and forgo the state match without increasing the backlog.

INTRODUCTION

The major highways and bridges damaged during Hurricane Irene in 2011 and the I-35W Minneapolis bridge collapse of August 1, 2007, are examples of disaster damaged federal-aid highway infrastructure that are eligible for assistance from the Emergency Relief Program (ER) of the Federal Highway Administration (FHWA). ER assistance is restricted to roads and bridges on the federal-aid highway system, which essentially includes all public roads not functionally classified as either local or rural minor collectors. For disaster-damaged roads that are not federal-aid highways, states may request reimbursement for emergency road repairs and debris removal from the Federal Emergency Management Agency (FEMA). FEMA may also allow for limited funding under its Public Assistance Program for such things as snow removal and related operating costs during extreme snowfalls, which are not eligible for ER funds.[1]

This report describes FHWA assistance for the repair and reconstruction of disaster-damaged highways and bridges or catastrophic failures (such as a bridge collapse). It begins with a brief discussion of the legislative origins of federal assistance and describes the ER program in its current form. The report then discusses eligibility issues and program operation.

BACKGROUND

For more than 70 years, federal aid has been available for the emergency repair and restoration of disaster-damaged roads. The first legislation authorizing such use of federal funds was the Hayden-Cartwright Act of 1934 (P.L. 73-393). This act, however, provided no separate funds and states subject to disasters had to divert their regularly apportioned federal highway funds from other uses to disaster repairs.

The Federal-Aid Highway and Highway Revenue Act of 1956 (70 Stat 374 and 70 Stat 387) was the first act that authorized separate funds for the ER program (the program is codified 23 U.S.C. 125). From the passage of the 1956 Act through 1978, funding for the program was drawn 40% from the Treasury's general fund revenues and 60% from the highway trust fund (HTF). The HTF is supported by taxes paid by highway users. Starting in 1979 the program was funded 100% from the HTF. The ER program was reauthorized, on August 10, 2005, through FY2009 by the Safe, Accountable, Flexible, Efficient Transportation Equity Act: A Legacy for Users (SAFETEA) (P.L. 109-59; 119 Stat 1144). SAFETEA provided that allocations above the annual $100 million authorization could be funded from the general fund.[2] Since the end of FY2009, the entire federal surface transportation program, including ER, has operated under a series of authorization extensions and continuing resolutions.[3]

FHWA'S EMERGENCY RELIEF (ER) PROGRAM

The ER program provides funds for the repair and reconstruction of roads on the federal-aid highway system that have suffered serious damage as a result of either (1) a natural disaster over a wide area, such as a flood, hurricane, tidal wave, earthquake, tornado, severe storm, or landslide; or (2) a catastrophic failure from any external cause (for example, the collapse of a bridge that is struck by a barge).[4] Historically, however, the vast majority of ER funds have gone for repair and reconstruction following natural disasters.

The Federal-State Relationship

As is true with other FHWA programs, the ER program is administered through the state departments of transportation in close coordination with FHWA's division offices in each state. Although the ER is a federal program, the decision to seek financial assistance under the program is made by the state departments of transportation, not by the federal government. Local officials who wish to seek ER funding must do so through their state departments of transportation. They do not deal directly with the FHWA. The close working relationships between FHWA staff at the state level and their state counterparts facilitate a quick coordinated response to disasters.

Funding

The ER program has an annual authorization of $100 million in contract authority to be derived from the highway trust fund. These funds are not subject to the obligation limitation, which means the entire $100 million is available each year. Because the costs of road repair and reconstruction following many disasters exceed the $100 million annual authorization, SAFETEA authorizes the appropriation of additional funds on a "such sums as may be necessary" basis, generally accomplished in either annual or emergency supplemental appropriations legislation.[5]

As is true with other FHWA programs, the ER is a reimbursable program. The state does not receive the money up front. This means, however, that a state can incur obligations and begin repairs knowing that it can submit vouchers to FHWA for reimbursement of the federal share of the project.

The $100 Million Per State Cap

The ER program limits the amount that FHWA may provide under the ER program to each state for each natural disaster or catastrophic failure to $100 million. For large disasters whose costs exceed the $100 million per state cap, Congress may lift the cap legislatively. This is often done at the same time that additional funds are appropriated for the program.

The Federal Share

Emergency repairs to restore essential travel, minimize the extent of damage, or protect remaining facilities, if accomplished within the first 180 days after the disaster, may be reimbursed with a 100% federal share.

Permanent repair projects are reimbursed at the same federal share that would normally apply to the federal-aid highway facility. For Interstate System highways the federal share would be 90% and for most other highways the share would be 80%. Permanent repairs done during the first 180 days are also reimbursed at the pro rata share that would normally apply to the facility. The share for disaster relief for roads on federal lands is 100%. In P.L. 109-148, Congress broadened the scope of the 100% federal share to encompass all ER program expenses for repair and reconstruction projects related to the Gulf Coast hurricanes. The I-35W repair and reconstruction, authorized in P.L. 110-56, was also 100% federally funded.

Eligibility and Program Operation

The ER program divides all repair work into two categories: emergency repairs and permanent repairs. Only repairs to roads and bridges on the federal-aid highway system that have suffered damage during a declared disaster or catastrophic failure are eligible for ER assistance.[6] The intent of ER assistance is to repair and restore highway facilities to pre-disaster conditions, not to increase capacity, improve highway facilities, or fix non-disaster deficiencies. In regard to bridges, ER funds are not to be used to replace other federal funds that would have been used to construct a replacement bridge (i.e., if replacement were already planned prior to the disaster). In general, work is confined to the federal-aid highway right-of-way.

Emergency Repairs

These are repairs made immediately following a disaster to meet the program goals to "restore essential traffic, to minimize the extent of damage, or to protect the remaining facilities."[7] State and local transportation agencies can begin these repairs immediately and prior approval from FHWA is not required. Once the FHWA division administrator finds that the disaster work is eligible, properly documented costs can be reimbursed retrospectively. Emergency repair work is to be accomplished within the first 180 days after the disaster and, as mentioned earlier, is reimbursed at a 100% federal share. Examples of emergency repairs are debris removal, regrading, removal of landslides, construction of temporary road detours, erection of temporary detour bridges, and use of ferries as an interim substitute for highway or bridge service. Emergency repairs are meant to permit work to start immediately to restore essential traffic in the disaster area that cannot wait for a finding of eligibility and programming of a project. This part of the program is especially designed for speed. In the case of some disasters, state DOTs have been able to let ER-funded debris removal and demolition contracts on the day of the disaster event.[8]

Permanent Repairs

Permanent repairs go beyond the restoration of essential traffic and are intended to restore the damaged bridges and roads to pre-disaster conditions and capabilities. Where the damaged parts of the road can be repaired to pre-disaster conditions, without replacement or reconstruction, this is done. Where a road needs to be replaced, ER funding is limited to the costs of building a roadway designed to current standards and of comparable capacity. ER funds may be used for temporary or permanent repair of a repairable bridge, but permanent repairs may not be funded if the bridge is scheduled for replacement. If a bridge is destroyed or repair is not feasible then ER funds may participate in building a new comparable bridge to current design standards and to accommodate traffic volume projected over its design life. In some cases "betterments" (added protective features, added lanes, added access control, etc.) may be eligible, but they must be shown to be economically justified based on a cost/benefit analysis of the future savings in recurring repair costs.

Permanent repair and reconstruction contracts, not done as emergency repairs, must meet competitive bidding requirements. A number of techniques are available to accelerate projects, including design-build contracting, abbreviated plans, shortened advertisement period for bids, and the cost-plus-time (A+B) bidding[9] that includes monetary incentive/disincentive clauses designed to encourage contractors to complete projects ahead of time. For example, the repair contract for repair of the I-10 Twin Spans Bridge between Slidell and New Orleans, Louisiana, that was awarded Friday September 9, 2005, included incentives for early completion. Two-way traffic on two lanes opened on October 14, 2005, 16 days ahead of schedule, and four-lane traffic opened January 6, 2006, nine days ahead of schedule. The contract for the replacement bridge for the collapsed I-35W bridge in Minneapolis also used incentives for early completion. The bridge was built in 11 months and was completed three months ahead of schedule.[10]

Contracts supported by ER funding must meet all contract provisions as required by 23 CFR Part 633A. Davis-Bacon wage rate requirements apply to all ER contracts.[11] ER-funded contracts must abide by Disadvantaged Business Enterprises (DBE) requirements, Americans With Disability Act (ADA) requirements, "buy America" regulations, and prohibitions against the use of convict labor (23 U.S.C. 114).[12]

Repair projects funded under the ER program are subject to the requirement of the National Environmental Policy Act (NEPA) of 1969. The impact, however, is generally limited since emergency repairs are normally classified as categorical exclusions under 23 CFR771.117 (c)(9) as are projects to permanently restore an existing facility "in-kind" to its pre-disaster condition. Betterments may, in some cases, require NEPA review.[13]

ER FUNDING SUSTAINABILITY

In February 2007, GAO released a report on the ER program that expressed concerns on the growing budgetary implications of ER spending.[14] The report points out that because of the constrained outlook for the highway trust fund, the ER program is now mostly funded with general fund revenues at a time when the

> nation faces a pending fiscal crisis, raising concerns about future use of the general fund and the financial sustainability of the ER program ... ER funds are not intended to replace other federal-aid, state, or local funds to increase capacity, correct nondisaster-related deficiencies, or make other improvements. However, contributing to future financial sustainability concerns is the fact that the scope of eligible activities funded by the ER program has expanded in recent years with congressional or FHWA waivers of eligibility criteria or changes in definitions. As a result, some projects have been funded that go beyond repairing or restoring highways to pre-disaster conditions ... [such as] projects that grew in scope and cost to address environmental and community concerns.... Congress has also directed that in some cases the program fully fund projects rather than requiring a state match.15

The report also noted that the $100 million annual authorization is so low, that since 1990, 86% of ER program funds have been made available though supplemental appropriations.

This situation has led to project backlogs that force states to delay reconstruction or use other highway dollars as they await the funds provided through the supplemental appropriations process.

RECENT "QUICK RELEASE" ER ALLOCATIONS

The *Emergency Relief Manual* describes the "quick release" method for developing and processing a state request for ER funding as a method which "employs a process to immediately deliver ER assistance for large disasters very quickly.

The quick release method should not be used as a matter of routine and is intended to provide a 'down payment' on overall ER needs immediately following a large scale disaster."[16]

- $2 million on September 14, 2011, to the State of Missouri for summer flood damage.
- $1 million on September 12, 2011, to the State of New Hampshire for flood damage from Hurricane Irene.
- $1 million on September 6, 2011, to the State of Maine for flood damage from Hurricane Irene.
- $1 million on September 2, 2011, to the State of Connecticut for flood damage from Hurricane Irene.
- $5 million on August 31, 2011, to the State of Vermont for flood damage from Hurricane Irene.
- $2 million on July 27, 2011, to the State of Iowa for flood damage.
- $5 million on June 27, 2011, to the State of North Dakota for flood damage.
- $1 million on May 24, 2011, to the State of Minnesota for flood damage from spring snow melt.

FY2011 NATIONWIDE ER ALLOCATIONS

On April 11, 2011, the FHWA allocated just under $320 million of ER funds to the states for reimbursement for repairs to damaged roads and bridges.[17]

Most of the funds were allocated to states for damage that occurred in 2010. Some funds were allocated for permanent repairs to earlier disasters.

I-35W MINNEAPOLIS BRIDGE ER FUNDING

Table 1 below, sets forth the allocation of ER funds for the reconstruction of the I-35W bridge, as of March 31, 2008.[18] As of this writing, the amount provided (allocated) equals the amount requested by the state of Minnesota.

Table 1. ER Funding for the I-35W Bridge Collapse

Funding Requests and Allocations	Amount
Total Formal Request for ER Funds	$371,700,000
"Quick Release" Allocation of August 2, 2007	$5,000,000
"Quick Release" Allocation of August 9, 2007	$50,000,000
Allocation of FY2008 ER funds on November 5, 2007	$123,482,833
Allocation of (P.L. 110-161) appropriation on March 5, 2008	$195,000,000
Total ER Funding for I-35W Bridge	$371,700,000

Source: DOT/FHWA.

Note: Simultaneously with the allocation of March 5, 2008, there was a withdrawal of $1,782,833 of previously allocated ER funds drawn from the annual ER authorization (i.e., which were not specifically appropriated for the I-35W bridge, as was the March 5 allocation, which was allocated in full).

2005 GULF COAST HURRICANE ER FUNDING

As of this writing, FHWA has received $2.950 billion in ER program funding requests and has allocated an equal amount for the repair and reconstruction of the damage to federal-aid highways caused by hurricanes Katrina, Rita, and Wilma. Table 2 presents the allocations of ER funding.

Table 2. 2005 Gulf Coast Hurricane ER Fund Allocations
(through March 31, 2010)

Item	Date	Amount Allocated ($)
Mississippi—Katrina	September 13, 2005	5,000,000
Louisiana—Katrina	September 14, 2005	5,000,000
Mississippi—Katrina	November 30, 2005	20,000,000
Louisiana—Katrina	November 30, 2005	20,000,000
Louisiana—Katrina	January 19, 2006	75,000,000
Florida—Katrina	January 20, 2006	42,843,797
Mississippi—Katrina	January 20, 2006	740,000,000

Table 2. (Continued)

Item	Date	Amount Allocated ($)
Texas—Rita	January 20, 2006	11,000,000
Louisiana—Katrina and Rita	February 1, 2006	863,001,488
Mississippi—Katrina	March 6, 2006	248,000,000
Alabama—Katrina	March 28, 2006	17,577,720
Florida—Rita	March 28, 2006	2,331,245
Florida—Wilma	March 28, 2006	478,000,000
Louisiana—Katrina and Rita	April 21, 2006	52,552,159
Louisiana—Katrina	July 13, 2006	174,000,000
Texas—Rita	October 23, 2006	25,994,607
Alabama—Katrina	July 24, 2007	9,800,000
Mississippi—Katrina	September 4, 2007	19,698,984
Mississippi—Katrina	September 4, 2007	301,016
Louisiana—Katrina	November 5, 2007	18,532,349
Louisiana—Katrina	October 23, 2008	3,025,475
Mississippi—Katrina	October 23, 2008	19,200,000
Texas—Rita	October 23, 2008	3,460,240
Mississippi—Katrina	November 5, 2008	4,800,000
Mississippi—Katrina	July 6, 2009	17,000,000
Louisiana—Katrina	March 31, 2010	74,500,000
Total		2,950,619,080

Source: FHWA.

End Notes

[1] Federal Highway Administration, Emergency Relief Manual (Federal-Aid Highways), Washington, DC, November 2009, p. 20, http://www.fhwa.dot.gov/reports/erm/er.pdf.

[2] Beginning with the December 30, 2005, enactment of the Emergency Supplemental Appropriations Act for Defense, the Global War on Terror, and Hurricane Recovery (P.L. 109-148), ER supplemental appropriations have been drawn from the Treasury's general fund.

[3] For background on surface transportation reauthorization issues see, CRS Report R41512, Surface Transportation Program Reauthorization Issues for the 112th Congress, coordinated by Robert S. Kirk.

[4] Federal Highway Administration, Emergency Relief Manual (Federal-Aid Highways), Washington, DC, November 2009, pp. 1-76, http://www.fhwa.dot.gov/reports/erm/er.pdf.

[5] Historically, emergency supplemental ER appropriations have been drawn from the highway account of the highway trust fund (HTF). The balance in the highway account had fallen in recent years and it was unclear whether the HTF could fund a large Katrina-related

supplemental appropriations without constraining the ability of the HTF to fully fund SAFETEA-LU. Since December 30, 2005, supplemental ER appropriations have come from the general fund.

[6] A governor may declare an emergency proclamation and the FHWA division administrator may then concur that a disaster occurred and substantial damage has occurred to the federal-aid highway system roads over a wide area or that the criteria for a catastrophic failure were met and that the damage is eligible under 23 U.S.C. 125. When the President has issued a major disaster declaration, the division administrator's concurrence is not necessary.

[7] FHWA. Emergency Relief Manual.

[8] A good example of this is the Northridge Earthquake. See Effects of Catastrophic Events on Transportation System Management and Operations, Washington, FHWA, 2004, pp. 37-45.

[9] Cost-plus-time bidding (A+B method) includes two components. The A component is the traditional bid for all work to be performed. The B component is a bid of the total number of calendar days required to complete the project. The contract includes a disincentive for overrunning the time bid and an incentive for earlier completion.

[10] Minnesota Department of Transportation, Interstate 35W Bridge in Minneapolis, Saint Paul, MN, http://www.dot.state.mn.us/i35wbridge/index.html.

[11] The Davis-Bacon requirements can be suspended by executive order (ref. 40 U.S.C. 276a-5). President Bush did this in response to Katrina. He reimposed the requirements November 8, 2005.

[12] A state may request a waiver of the buy America requirements from FHWA based on a public interest rationale under 23 CFR 635.4109(c)(1)(i).

[13] CRS Report RL33104, NEPA and Hurricane Response, Recovery, and Rebuilding Efforts, by Linda Luther.

[14] U.S. Government Accountability Office, Highway Emergency Relief: Reexamination Needed to Address Fiscal Imbalance and Long-term Sustainability, GAO-07-245, February 2007, pp. 1-60, http://www.gao.gov/new.items/ d07245.pdf.

[15] Ibid. p. 2.

[16] Federal Highway Administration. Office of Infrastructure, Emergency Relief Manual, Washington, DC, November 2009, p. 33, http://www.fhwa.dot.gov/reports /erm/ermchap3. cfm.

[17] Federal Highway Administration, "U.S. Secretary of Transportation Announces More than $319 Million as Repayment for Repairs to Damaged Roads and Bridges," press release, March 31, 2011, http://www.fhwa.dot.gov/pressroom/dot11045.htm.

[18] See also CRS Report RL34127, Highway Bridges: Conditions and the Federal/State Role, by Robert S. Kirk and William J. Mallett.

In: Federal Programs and Policies for Highways   ISBN: 978-1-62257-755-2
Editors: E.D. Campbell and E.Sanchez © 2013 Nova Science Publishers, Inc.

Chapter 5

TOLLING OF INTERSTATE HIGHWAYS: ISSUES IN BRIEF[*]

Robert S. Kirk

INTRODUCTION

The prohibition of tolling of federal-aid highways dates back to the Federal Road Act of 1916 (39 Stat. 355). Subsequent legislation modified the prohibition to the point where now the only significant part of the federal-aid highway system under the toll prohibition is the Interstate Highway System, comprising approximately 47,000 miles of the roughly 1-million-mile federal-aid highway system. Congress, in approving the Federal-Aid Highway Act and Highway Revenue Act of 1956 (P.L. 84-621; 70 Stat. 374), rejected the use of tolls or user fees to finance construction in favor of creating a highway trust fund supported by dedicated fuel taxes. However, certain existing expressway segments that were incorporated into the Interstate Highway System already had tolls in 1956, and they are not covered by the tolling prohibition.

In recent years the revenues flowing into the highway trust fund have been insufficient to maintain even current levels of federal funding for highways. Political resistance to raising the federal fuels tax is high. The fuel taxes

---

[*] This is an edited, reformatted and augmented version of a Congressional Research Service publication, CRS Report for Congress R42402, from www.crs.gov, prepared for Members and Committees of Congress, dated March 12, 2012.

dedicated to the highway trust fund, currently 18.3 cents per gallon of gasoline and 24.3 cents per gallon of diesel fuel, were last raised in 1993.

Historically, interest in toll financing has increased during periods of constrained federal funding. Since the Interstate Highways make up nearly all federal-aid highway segments that are still under the tolling prohibition, advocates of expanded use of tolling focus their efforts on giving states more flexibility to impose tolls on the Interstates within their borders.

PROS AND CONS[1]

The arguments in favor of expanding tolling of the Interstate Highways include the following:

- The Interstate Highway System includes many of the corridors with the level of traffic that makes the best business sense for toll-supported public-private partnerships and other forms of alternative finance, which could use the tolls along with other sources of revenue to finance roadway improvements.
- The Interstate highways and bridges are nearly all 50 years old and need to be rebuilt at many times their original cost. Given the insufficiency of the revenues flowing into the highway trust fund and constrained state budgets, states need to be able to use tolling to rebuild the Interstate Highways.
- Allowing the broader use of tolling on urban Interstates could increase the use of road pricing to reduce congestion and also provide revenue for maintenance or reconstruction of urban interstates.
- Tolling of the Interstates gives drivers the choice of paying or not paying for the upkeep of the tolled Interstate segment by choosing to pay the toll or using an alternative route.
- Tolling of the Interstates will allow states to reconstruct them sooner than they would otherwise be able.
- Tolling advocates also argue that tolling can improve the efficiency of investment, because in order to attract private capital the toll facility must meet the market test of offering a competitive rate of return.

Arguments in opposition to tolling of the Interstate Highways include the following:

- Such a policy would overturn the "freedom from tolls" provision of the 1956 act, and might be open to criticism that tolling of roads that were built or improved with revenues from highway user taxes is double taxation.
- Much of the Interstate System may not be suitable for tolling. For tolling to make economic sense, the traffic on the toll facility must be sufficient to cover costs and, in the case of public-private partnerships, to provide for a reasonable profit.
- Some argue that tolls increase costs and place a burden on interstate commerce.
- Most of the Interstate System is rural and tolling these routes may not be feasible.
- Tolls are seen as regressive and disproportionately impacting low-income drivers.
- States are likely to neglect the competing free roads once they commit to the toll facility.
- Most proposals for tolling of the Interstate Highways envision continued federal financial participation, but this should be unnecessary if tolling of an Interstate Highway segment truly makes economic sense.

POLICY CHOICES

Advocates of tolling would make more or all Interstate Highway System segments eligible for conversion to toll roads. The Interstates carry high traffic volumes relative to other roads and are often congested in urban areas. About 7% of the 16,555 miles of urban Interstates are currently tolled.

Both of the commissions established under Safe, Accountable, Flexible, Efficient Transportation Equity Act: a Legacy for Users (SAFETEA; P.L. 109-59)[2] recommended allowing expanded tolling of Interstate Highways. This could be done in a number of ways, including changing the law to allow the imposition of tolls at state discretion; or making permanent existing pilot programs involving tolling, including the Value Pricing Program, the Express Lane Demonstration program, the Interstate System Reconstruction and

Rehabilitation Pilot Program, and the Interstate System Construction Toll Pilot Program.[3]

The policy choice is not all or nothing. One possibility would be to allow the tolling of urban Interstate Highways only. However, this could lead to a difference in Interstate Highway funding between more densely populated urban areas that rely on tolling while sparsely populated rural areas remain dependent on federal grants. This could weaken support for federal-aid highway grants by urban interests who might see the grants as primarily benefiting rural areas.

Recently, two other issues related to tolling of the Interstate Highways have surfaced that could have a major impact on the acceptance or rejection of tolling the Interstate Highways. These issues deal with how and on whom the tolls would be imposed, if tolling of the Interstate Highways is expanded.

Collecting Tolls at State Borders

Officials from some of the states that have expressed interest in the Interstate System Reconstruction & Rehabilitation Pilot Program have proposed in public statements collecting the tolls on the converted segments of Interstate Highway at state borders. This would shift much of the toll burden onto interstate travelers or shippers, while leaving many intra-state trips along the same highways toll-free. Tolling supporters in these states see border tolls as both a way of shifting the costs of "pass through" traffic to out-of-state travelers and shippers and a way to make tolling of the routes more acceptable to their states' residents.

Border tolling raises a number of policy issues at the federal level. One is whether it is appropriate for a federal program to support conversion of a "free" Interstate Highway, bridge, or tunnel to a toll facility whose costs are borne primarily by interstate travel and shipping. In a broader sense, should the Interstate Highway system be opened up to tolling, border tolling could become the norm as states respond to border tolls set by adjacent states by setting their own border tolls; "toll wars" between states are not unimaginable. Finally, some say, border tolling may contravene the Commerce Clause of the Constitution, which reserved the power to "regulate commerce with foreign nations, and among the several states" to Congress.

In a practical sense, depending on border tolls and giving intra-state users a free ride could have a major negative impact on the revenue potential of the toll conversion. This collection regime also is one that is relatively easy to bypass, as many state border crossings have competing non-Interstate highway roads.

Setting Different Rates for Interstate and Local Toll Facility Users

Officials in some states have suggested a two-tier tolling system, with lower toll charges for instate residents and higher charges on interstate users. To date, the variable charges have mostly been imposed on bridges, which, unlike federal-aid highways, are not subject to Federal Highway Administration toll regulation.[4] Electronic toll collection makes the segmenting of toll facility users into out-of-state, in-state, or local categories feasible. As is true with border tolling, different tolls for intra-state and interstate users may invoke issues related to the Commerce Clause.[5] If reauthorization legislation includes provisions to expand tolling of Interstate Highways, the tolling of out-of-state versus in-state users will likely be a significant issue.

End Notes

[1] See Ed Regan and Steven Brown, "Building the Case for Tolling the Interstates," Tollways, spring 2011, reprint pp. 1- 10; Beth Pinkston, Toll Roads: a Review of Recent Experience,: Congressional Budget Office, February 1997, pp. 1-6; U.S. Government Accountability Office, Road Pricing Can Help Reduce Congestion, but Equity Concerns May Grow, Washington, GAO, "GAO-12-119," pp. 1-33; William Reinhardt, "The Role of Private Investment in Meeting U.S. Transportation Infrastructure Needs," Public Works Financing, v. 260, May 2011, p. 9; Alan van der Hilst, Using Public-Private Partnerships to Carry Out Highway Projects, Congressional Budget Office, January 2012, pp. 1-32.

[2] National Surface Transportation Policy and Revenue Study Commission, Transportation for Tomorrow: Final Report, Chapter 5, http://mtcfilehost.net/transportationfortomorrow /final_report/pdf/volume_2_chapter_5.pdf. The study estimated that aggressive use of tolling opportunities in SAFETEA could generate $8.9 billion in additional revenue between FY2007 and FY2017. See also National Surface Transportation Infrastructure Financing Commission, Paying Our Way: a New Framework for Transportation Finance, Final Report, February 26, 2009, pp. 28, 25-36, 207, http://financecommission.dot .gov/Documents/ NSTIF_Commission_Final_Report_ Mar09 FNL.pdf.

[3] "The Role of Private Investment in Meeting U.S. Transportation Infrastructure Needs," Public Works Financing, May 2011, p. 9.

[4] Section 135 of the Surface Transportation and Uniform Relocation Assistance Act of 1987 (P.L. 100-17) repealed the Department of Transportation's (DOT's) authority to regulate tolls on

bridges. Bridge tolls were required to be "just and reasonable" but were no longer subject to regulation by DOT.

[5] See "On Tolls, Transponders, and the Constitution's Commerce Clause," Wall Street Journal, April 2, 2009; "Rhode Island Bridge Defeats Law Suit Claiming Unconstitutionality of Residence Discount," Tollroads News, April 7, 2011, http://www.tollroadsnews. com/node/5254. Reportedly, the Rhode Island Bridge Authority and the plaintiff agreed that in return for not appealing the decision, the Bridge Authority would pay some of the plaintiff's litigation costs. See also "Possible Commerce Clause Claims Related to State Tolling of Existing Interstates," Truckline, http://www.trudkline.com/Federation/S TA/ Documents/CONSITIUTIONAL%20claims.pdf.

In: Federal Programs and Policies for Highways   ISBN: 978-1-62257-755-2
Editors: E.D. Campbell and E.Sanchez © 2013 Nova Science Publishers, Inc.

Chapter 6

PLANNING AND FLEXIBILITY ARE KEY TO EFFECTIVELY DEPLOYING BROADBAND CONDUIT THROUGH FEDERAL HIGHWAY PROJECTS[*]

The United States Government Accountability Office

The Honorable Henry A. Waxman
Ranking Member
Committee on Energy and Commerce House of Representatives

The Honorable Anna G. Eshoo
Ranking Member
Subcommittee on Communications and Technology
Committee on Energy and Commerce
House of Representatives

The Honorable Edward J. Markey
The Honorable Doris O. Matsui
House of Representatives

Affordable access to broadband telecommunications is increasingly viewed as vital to the country's economic growth as well as for improving

---

[*] This is an edited, reformatted and augmented version of The United States Government Accountability Office publication, dated June 27, 2012.

state and local systems for traffic management, public safety, and educational goals.[1] According to the Federal Communications Commission (FCC), the largest cost element for deploying broadband via fiber optic cable is the cost of placement, such as burying the fiber in the ground, rather than the cost of the fiber itself. Recent legislation introduced in both the U.S. Senate and House of Representatives would require the Secretary of Transportation to require states to install broadband conduit during construction for certain federally funded highway projects in compliance with standards developed by the Secretary, in coordination with FCC.[2] Both the House and Senate bills would make conduit available to any requesting broadband service provider for a "charge not to exceed a cost-based rate." Both bills would affect only new construction or highway expansion projects that receive federal funding and would not, for example, affect projects limited to road resurfacing or general maintenance.

You requested that we examine proposed federal "dig once" policies that would require the deployment of broadband conduit in conjunction with federally funded highway construction projects as a way to decrease the costs of deploying fiber and eliminate the need for multiple excavations.[3] This report presents information on (1) the advantages and disadvantages of dig once policies and (2) how the broadband deployment experiences of states and localities that have implemented dig once policies can inform the consideration of a federal dig once policy.

SCOPE AND METHODOLOGY

This information is based on our analysis of documents from and interviews with officials from FCC; the Federal Highway Administration (FHWA); state departments of transportation in California, Massachusetts, Michigan, Oregon, Utah, and Virginia; associations including the Telecommunications Industry Association, the National Association of Telecommunications Officers and Advisors, the National Association of Regulatory Utility Commissioners, the American Association of State Highway and Transportation Officials, the New America Foundation, the California Emerging Technology Fund, and the Massachusetts Broadband Institute; providers of broadband service and infrastructure including Google, Verizon, Inyo Networks, Sonic.net, Monkeybrains, Slic Network Solutions, and Jaguar Communications; and local government agencies in San Francisco, California; Santa Monica, California; Burbank, California; and Portland, Oregon. State departments of transportation and local government agencies were selected based on recommendations from U.S. Department of Transportation (DOT) and FCC officials and others we spoke with during the course of our work because of their experience with dig once or similar policies. Broadband service and infrastructure providers were selected to achieve a diversity of viewpoints, sizes, and company types. Our selection of stakeholders was judgmental and thus, responses are not generalizable but provide key insights into the experiences of state and local governments and others with experience deploying broadband conduit and networks.

We conducted this performance audit from December 2011 through June 2012 in accordance with generally accepted government auditing standards. Those standards require that we plan and perform the audit to obtain sufficient, appropriate evidence to provide a reasonable basis for our findings and conclusions based on our audit objectives. We believe that the evidence obtained provides a reasonnable basis for our findings and conclusions based on our audit objectives.

RESULTS IN BRIEF

A federal dig once policy would likely have several advantages, including potentially decreasing the frequency of construction on major highways and the cost of installation, while accelerating access to and reliability of broadband networks. However, disadvantages—which could be exacerbated by a requirement to install conduit as part of certain federally funded highway construction—include the potential to install conduit that telecommunications companies might not use and to divert highway funding away from highway construction. DOT, FCC, and state DOT officials we spoke with supported the concept of a dig once policy, but suggested alternative approaches to a federal requirement to install conduit in all covered projects. For example, FCC officials expressed support for a federal requirement for evaluation of the feasibility and need for conduit during federal highway construction, and state and U.S. DOT officials expressed support for a federal role in facilitating discussion and best practice sharing among states implementing broadband deployment policies.

State and local broadband deployment experiences demonstrate the importance of planning and flexibility to effectively implement dig once policies. Officials from states and localities we spoke with have adopted various strategies—including establishing formal coordination processes between state DOTs and local utility companies—but none required installation of conduit as part of all roadway construction. These officials stated that planning and coordination with local officials is a critical step to address a number of considerations that should be taken into account during implementation—such as the location of access points and the appropriate number and size of conduits—to make the conduit installed more useful for telecommunications companies. In addition, officials from states and telecommunication companies stated that the flexibility to take local needs into account in implementing a dig once policy on a project-byproject basis is important and may help to address the potential disadvantages of a federal dig once policy.

BACKGROUND

FCC regulates interstate and international communications by radio, television, wire, satellite, and cable. According to FCC, communications infrastructure has played a critical role in increasing opportunities for American innovation, industry, job growth, and international competitiveness. As such, FCC works to promote competition, innovation, and investment in broadband services and facilities.

Broadband access in the U.S. has thus far been driven largely by private investment and market innovations and has improved considerably in the last decade, but there are critical problems that slow the progress of availability, adoption, and utilization of broadband. Such problems include the high cost of deployment in some locations. To encourage further broadband deployment, FCC's National Broadband Plan recommends that Congress consider enacting dig once legislation applying to all future federally funded highway projects along rights-of-way and that the U.S. DOT make federal financing of highway, road, and bridge projects contingent on states and localities allowing joint deployment of conduits by qualified parties.[4]

Federal funding for highways is provided to the states primarily through grant programs collectively known as the Federal-Aid Highway Program. In a joint federal-state partnership, FHWA, a division within the U.S. DOT, administers the Federal-Aid Highway Program and distributes most of the funding to the states through annual apportionments established by statutory formulas. Once apportioned, the funds are available for obligation for construction, reconstruction, and improvement of highways on eligible routes. About 1 million of the nation's 4 million miles of roads are eligible for federal aid—including the 161,000-mile National Highway System.

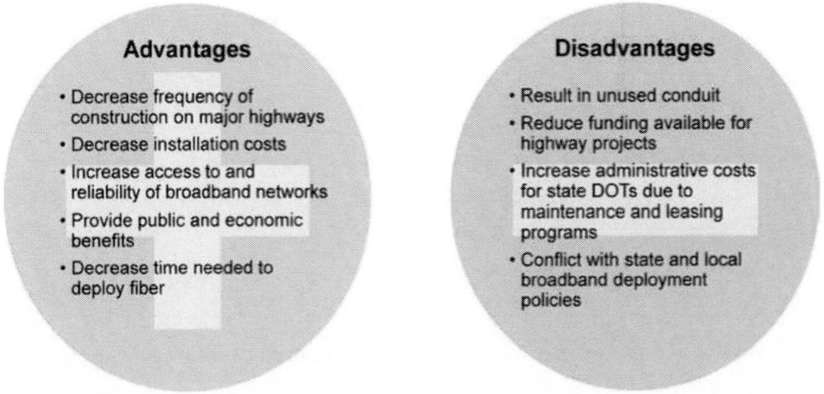

Advantages

- Decrease frequency of construction on major highways
- Decrease installation costs
- Increase access to and reliability of broadband networks
- Provide public and economic benefits
- Decrease time needed to deploy fiber

Disadvantages

- Result in unused conduit
- Reduce funding available for highway projects
- Increase administrative costs for state DOTs due to maintenance and leasing programs
- Conflict with state and local broadband deployment policies

Source: GAO.

Figure 1. Federal and State Officials' Views about Potential Advantages and Disadvantages of a Federal Dig Once Policy.

The responsibility for selecting specific highway projects generally rests with state DOTs and local planning organizations, which have discretion in determining how to allocate available federal funds among various eligible projects.

Fiber optic cables provide extremely fast data transmission speeds and are commonly used for long haul transmissions, such as the Internet backbone and middle mile.[5] Fiber optic technology converts electronic signals carrying data to light, sends the light through transparent glass or plastic fibers about the diameter of a human hair, and converts the light back to electronic form for delivery.

These fibers are combined into cable of various size diameters, and these cables are then commonly buried inside an underground conduit where they are better protected from the elements or natural disasters.

Depending on traffic demand, fiber optic technology may be deployed from the provider's facilities to a customer's home or business. In many instances, the part of the connection to the customer's premises, commonly called "the last mile," may be provided over coaxial cable, copper loop, or wireless technology, which may be more cost-effective than a total fiber connection.

Industry documentation estimates that the expected useful life of fiber cables is between 20 and 25 years and that the expected useful life of underground conduit is between 25 and 50 years. Current dig once policy proposals are focused on increasing middle-mile and backbone broadband infrastructure rather than last-mile fiber infrastructure to homes and businesses.

A FEDERAL DIG ONCE POLICY HAS SEVERAL POTENTIAL ADVANTAGES AND DISADVANTAGES

Federal and state officials and industry representatives we spoke with described the potential advantages and disadvantages associated with federal dig once policies (see figure 1). While the potential advantages apply to dig once policies in general, some potential disadvantages may be more or less applicable depending on the specific elements of a federal dig once policy.

Potential Advantages

- *Decrease frequency of construction on major highways.* Combining broadband conduit installation with highway construction, rather than installing the conduit at a later date, might result in fewer construction-related disturbances on federal-aid highways. Decreasing the number of times a roadway is under construction should decrease construction-related traffic congestion and could potentially increase the life-span of roadways, as frequent construction can reduce the integrity of road materials.

- *Decrease installation costs.* The cost to install underground conduit for broadband deployment varies, but installation costs could decrease in some cases if conduit is installed during road construction projects because of the ability to share those costs with others involved in the road project. One industry official stated that cost savings would depend on the type of work being completed for the principal highway project. If the highway project includes, for example, digging trenches for water mains or other facilities, then trenching equipment will be on site and available and the costs for that equipment would be shared among the broadband, water, and other portions of the project. Officials we spoke with noted that the amount of cost savings also depends on the type of terrain in which the conduit is installed and the installation method required. For example, for a 2011 broadband deployment project through portions of California and Nevada, the average contractor bid was $2.18 per linear foot for "plowing"[6] in dirt and $10.86 per linear foot for "trenching"[7] in dirt. For the same project, the average contractor bid for installing conduit by "boring"[8] was about $22 per linear foot in dirt but about $108 per linear foot in areas with solid rock. Taking these factors into consideration, some of the state officials we spoke with reported that coordinating road work and underground conduit deployment in their states had resulted in cost savings. For instance, officials from one state DOT as well as an engineering assessment commissioned for the city of San Francisco estimate that when conduit and fiber installation is coordinated with a road or utility project, savings range from 25-33 percent and are greatest in densely populated areas where the complexity and cost of construction is highest. Similarly, Utah DOT, in comparing two rural broadband deployment projects, estimated cost savings of roughly 15.5 percent per mile when conduit and fiber were installed during a road project rather than being installed independent of a road project.

- Increase access to and reliability of broadband networks. Officials stated that dig once policies could increase access to and reliability of broadband networks at a faster rate than current deployment efforts. For example, dig once policies could provide telecommunications companies with access to lower cost state-owned conduit in rural areas, thus encouraging them to build out their networks in those areas. Further, installing additional conduit in areas that already have broadband access could improve network reliability by providing redundancy in cases of damage by natural disasters, sabotage, or construction. Additionally, officials stated that dig once policies can provide an opportunity to replace aging or aerial infrastructure (such as underground copper infrastructure or fiber attached to telephone poles) with underground conduit, which is less susceptible to damage.

- *Provide public and economic benefits.* Officials we spoke with stated that a dig once or similar policy could lead to various public and economic benefits. First, officials from some state DOTs, local governments, and industry organizations stated that a dig once policy could assist states and localities in developing intelligent transportation[9] and public safety systems by making conduit available for state and local use. Officials in some localities also stated that access to locally owned conduit has reduced local government telecommunications costs. Second, some officials stated that a dig once policy might lead to decreases in broadband prices and/or increased broadband performance for consumers because of potentially increased competition resulting from the availability of conduit open to all broadband providers. Third, officials in some localities as well as industry stakeholders stated that increased access to broadband benefits existing businesses and could draw new businesses to the area, both of which could increase local economic activity.

- *Decrease time needed to deploy fiber.* Some officials we spoke to stated that, depending on implementation, a dig once policy has the potential to decrease the time it takes to deploy fiber by reducing the legal and regulatory steps associated with activities such as environmental impact studies and obtaining permits in multiple jurisdictions. For instance, if companies have access to state-owned conduit, they may be able to deploy fiber through that conduit without completing steps such as environmental impact studies, which would have been completed at the time of conduit installation.

POTENTIAL DISADVANTAGES

- *Result in unused conduit.* Most officials we spoke with stated that a dig once policy that included a federal mandate to install conduit could result in miles of unused conduit and wasted funds. For example, while installing conduit for Virginia DOT use in 1998, the agency installed spare conduit in a major highway interchange with the intent to lease it to generate revenue and to avoid additional construction by telecommunications companies. Officials told us that local telecommunications companies were not interested in leasing the conduit because their customer base in the area—largely U.S. government agencies and contractors—often requires carriers to own their infrastructure rather than lease infrastructure. According to Virginia DOT officials, it took 10 years for the agency to generate revenue from the extra conduit by selling portions of the conduit system in 2008 and 2011. Officials at Caltrans, California's DOT, told us that the agency had a similar experience with conduit installed in the 1990s that remains unused. Further, while some officials stated that short pieces of installed conduit can prove to be useful, others were concerned that many current highway projects are completed over distances of 1 or 2 miles. A mandate to install conduit with federal highway projects could result in small segments of conduit across the country that do not connect to other broadband infrastructure. Additionally, industry and other officials stated that it may take many years for companies to develop a need for the conduit installed as a result of dig once policies. With no active fiber inside the conduit to provide incentive for states and companies to protect conduit from road work and other hazards, officials were concerned that the conduit might become damaged and unusable.

- *Reduce funding available for highway projects.* While the costs of conduit installation are small relative to the costs of most highway projects, a dig once policy could reduce funding available for highway projects at a time when most state DOTs are struggling financially. For example, according to Utah DOT officials, broadband conduit and fiber installation comprised approximately 7 percent of the total budget for a 19.36-mile road construction project in Utah. Unless an alternative funding source were established, the incremental costs of conduit installation and conduit management would be borne by either state DOT budgets or federal-aid highway funding, thus reducing the amount of funding available for the principal mission of the project: highway construction. While leasing programs may help states recover these costs, states will be responsible for the costs of conduit installation and administration until the conduit becomes used by telecommunications companies. Additionally, state DOT and U.S. DOT officials stated that broadband conduit design and construction could delay the design and completion of highway projects.

- *Increase administrative costs for state DOTs and local governments due to maintenance and leasing programs.* In addition to the costs of installation, some officials expressed concern about the costs to maintain the conduit, maintain a conduit inventory, and administer a leasing program, all of which may require additional personnel. In states and localities we spoke to, additional personnel have been hired in order to manage leasing programs and maintenance, such as might be required under a federal dig once policy. For instance, Utah DOT employs one full-time employee in addition to contract support to manage the agency's fiber optic program. Similarly, the city of Santa Monica, California, employs three full time employees to manage the technical and marketing aspects of its broadband program, and has begun working with a contractor to assist with administering the network.

- *Conflict with state and local broadband deployment policies.* State and local officials raised concerns about a federal dig once policy and cost-based rate requirement affecting states' ability to continue current broadband deployment programs. For example, Utah DOT officials expressed concern that a requirement to install conduit and lease it at a cost-based rate would prohibit Utah's current broadband deployment efforts in which the state trades the use of excess state-owned conduit and fiber for access to conduit owned by telecommunications companies.[10] Similarly, Massachusetts DOT (MassDOT) officials stated concerns that a requirement to lease conduit at a cost-based rate would prohibit the state's current practice of charging market-based leasing fees to companies that place fiber infrastructure in the state's right-of-way, resulting in the loss of a revenue stream. U.S. DOT officials also noted that some states restrict the use of transportation funding for utilities infrastructure, a restriction that may conflict with a federal dig once policy.

FCC officials stated that the agency has not conducted any studies on dig once policies or implemented policies similar to dig once, but that the agency generally supports a federal dig once policy. FCC officials further stated that they would support a dig once policy that requires an evaluation of the feasibility and need for broadband conduit as a part of the highway construction process, rather than a mandate to install conduit in all covered projects. While DOT does not currently have any programs or policies that promote dig once or similar broadband deployment strategies, DOT has expressed support for developing a dig once policy and noted that current regulations allow for fiber optic cable to be run lengthwise along highway rights-ofHowever, if a way[11] federal dig once policy were implemented, DOT officials expressed concern that the agency would be making decisions and setting policy outside of its scope of expertise, which is focused on transportation, rather than broadband deployment. Additionally, DOT officials stated that a dig once policy applying to federally funded new construction and expansion highway projects would likely affect a very small percentage of the nation's roadways. While approximately 30 percent of all federal-aid highway program funding is allocated annually toward reconstruction and widening improvement projects, this funding is spent on about 4 percent of the National Highway System, or approximately .01 percent of the nation's roads open to public travel.[12]

Some state DOT officials we contacted suggested that, rather than a federal dig once policy, U.S. DOT and FCC should act as facilitators to assist states in creating broadband deployment policies. For instance, officials in one state suggested that US DOT facilitate a workshop in which state DOTs with established broadband policies share best practices and ideas with other states. The U.S. DOT officials we spoke with expressed support for this type of facilitation, rather than legislation linking federal highway funding to deployment of broadband conduit. On June 14, 2012, the President issued Executive Order 13616,[13] "Accelerating Broadband Infrastructure Deployment," that, among other activities, requires that the U.S. DOT do the following:

- Implement a flexible set of best practices that can accommodate changes in broadband technology and minimize excavations consistent with competitive broadband deployment.
- Work with state and local governments to help them develop and implement best practices on establishing dig once requirements, effectively using private investment in state intelligent transportation infrastructure, and other related activities.

BROADBAND DEPLOYMENT EXPERIENCES ILLUSTRATE THE BENEFITS OF PLANNING AND FLEXIBILITY

Officials from states and localities we spoke with have had a variety of broadband deployment experiences and have adopted various strategies to promote broadband deployment and infrastructure.

Some have implemented dig once policies that encourage coordination between transportation agencies and utility companies to prevent additional road construction, but we did not identify any states or localities that have dig once policies that require installation of conduit as part of any road construction project.

State and local strategies include formal coordination policies between state DOTs and utility companies, a system of trading the use of state-owned conduit for use of conduit owned by telecommunications companies, and city-owned fiber optic networks, among others.

For example:

- Michigan DOT has implemented a formal coordination process in which the DOT provides its future road work plans to local utility companies, giving the companies an opportunity to complete work while the DOT has roads under construction.
- Similarly, the city of San Francisco coordinates with local utility companies through its joint trenching policy, which allows utility companies to install conduit or perform maintenance either prior to or during roadway reconstruction and restoration. The policy includes a 5-year moratorium on excavating streets that have been reconstructed, repaved, or resurfaced.
- Utah DOT and Virginia DOT leverage private companies' assets to decrease the cost of expanding their state-owned fiber optic networks, which support their intelligent transportation systems, through a fiber optic resource sharing program and conduit trade system. Virginia's DOT allows private companies to install conduit and/or fiber in its limited access right-of-way, where it does not typically allow utility installations, in exchange for the use of company-owned conduit and/or fiber in areas where the state does not have broadband infrastructure. Utah DOT installs conduit for its own network—sometimes coordinating conduit installation with road construction—and allows private companies to use excess state-owned conduit in exchange for the use of company-owned conduit in areas where the state does not have broadband infrastructure.
- MassDOT views its highway right-of-way as an asset developed by the state and, correspondingly, charges telecommunications companies leasing fees for using it. Companies with underground fiber networks provide MassDOT with fiber or conduit space, and then the value of the fiber or conduit space is deducted from the company's leasing fee.
- Both Santa Monica and Burbank have city-owned fiber optic networks. The city of Burbank has deployed its network primarily through existing electrical conduit and generates nominal revenue for Burbank Water and Power by leasing excess capacity to local businesses. Santa Monica built its fiber optic network to reduce the city's costs associated with buying Internet service from a telecommunications company, enhance telecommunications services, and promote economic development. The city generates revenue through leasing

services to local businesses to support network operations and fund community programs.

PLANNING AND FLEXIBILITY ARE KEY TO SUCCESSFULLY IMPLEMENTING DIG ONCE POLICIES

State, local, and industry officials we contacted who have experience deploying broadband networks stated that planning is an important aspect of ensuring that a broadband deployment project is successful. For example, officials planned Digital 395, a 583-mile broadband deployment project located primarily along highway 395 in California and Nevada, for more than 2 years prior to breaking ground to install conduit. Planning steps included identifying levels of broadband service in the deployment area and the number of households and businesses located in the proposed service area. Additionally, recent federal programs that promote broadband deployment[14] have required grant and loan applicants to demonstrate planning and goal setting, including how the project will create sustainable broadband adoption in the target area, a project timeline that establishes key milestones for the implementation of the project, and potential challenges that could pose delays, among other information.

Officials stated that coordination between states and local communities is an important part of planning the deployment of broadband networks because local communities have a better understanding of their broadband needs than states or the federal government and working with local officials helps ensure that local requirements are met by the state.[15]

Additionally, a better understanding of the broadband needs in an area should help state DOTs determine which highway projects should include conduit. For example, some officials stated that interstate highways in the northeast U.S. typically have enough fiber optic infrastructure and that more conduit is not needed. Additionally, some areas may not need new conduit because there are alternative deployment methods. For example, Google officials stated that in a recent fiber deployment project in Kansas City, Kansas, Google deployed fiber optic cables through existing municipally owned utility conduit, so there was little need for additional conduit during the deployment process.

Officials stated that planning, including coordination with local officials, may help address several implementation considerations that should be taken into account for conduit installed under a dig once policy to be useful and appealing to telecommunications companies.

Leaving these considerations unaddressed may result in conduit that is poorly designed or managed. State DOT and other officials stated that if officials were tasked with implementation of a dig once policy, they should consider conduit access, installation, management, maintenance, and cost issues, including:

- *The location of access points along the conduit.* To allow for maintenance and the connection of customers to the fiber optic cable, there should be points along conduit at which fiber optic cable can be installed in the conduit and accessed in the future.
- *The number and size of conduits.* The number of conduits and size of conduit affect the number and strand count of fiber optic cables that can be installed in a single conduit or a bank of conduit. For example, if a state installs four 1-inch conduits, it likely means that the maximum amount of fiber optic cable the conduits can house is four half-inch fiber optic cables.
- *Security of conduit and access points.* Telecommunications officials stated that companies may not want to share conduit and access points with other companies because of security and safety concerns about their fiber optic cables being damaged by another party. Additionally, an official suggested that the creation of a qualified vendor list is needed to control who can access the conduit to pull fiber optic cable, perform maintenance, and prevent damage as a result of negligence.
- *The conduit allocation process.* The allocation of conduit between public and private entities needs to be managed to effectively give companies access to the conduit and to prevent misuse of the conduit. For example, some officials were concerned that large companies might be allowed to lease all excess conduit space in order to eliminate competition.
- *A conduit map.* A high-quality map or database displaying the location, number, and size of conduits is necessary for telecommunications companies to efficiently locate and access the conduit.
- *The management of right-of-way access.* Depending on how a policy is implemented, state-owned conduit could make the permitting and coordination process for accessing rights-ofway in different jurisdictions easier—by requiring that companies only coordinate with

the state DOT—or more difficult—by requiring that companies coordinate with all the jurisdictions the conduit crosses through.

- *The designation of conduit maintenance responsibilities.* The clear designation of maintenance responsibilities is important because maintenance can become complicated if conduit or fiber is damaged by an outside party, natural disaster, or another telecommunications company.
- *Setting conduit access rates.* The cost to lease conduit from the state must be reasonable and, if the conduit is leased at a cost-based rate, states should clearly delineate how costs would be allocated among users. For example, states should decide if the access rates will differ depending on the number of companies that are colocated in conduit. If one company has to bear all of the costs because it is the only company using the conduit, versus three companies sharing the cost of the conduit, telecommunications companies may be hesitant to be the first to lease conduit.

In addition to planning, state and telecommunications company officials stated that a dig once policy should allow for flexibility based on the needs of states and localities. Officials stated that flexibility is beneficial when deploying broadband infrastructure because different areas of the country have different needs, so conduit installation should be considered on a project-by-project basis. For example, some officials stated that it does not make sense to install conduit in a 5-mile stretch of road that is not close to other telecommunications infrastructure or if no work is planned on successive lengths of road in the near future. Additionally, it may be cost prohibitive to install conduit in some areas of the country where terrain is challenging. For example, the average contractor bid for boring in areas of solid rock was about five times the cost of directional boring in areas with mostly dirt for a 2011 broadband deployment project through portions of California and Nevada. Similarly, in rural areas, aerial installation allows for more flexibility to connect newly built homes to fiber optic cables than underground conduit, according to an official at a telecommunications company that specializes in providing broadband to rural areas.

However, officials told us that certain areas or projects would benefit greatly from pre-installed conduit, including bridges, interstate highway crossings, and highway interchanges. Officials stated that such projects can be difficult, costly, and even dangerous places to install conduit so preexisting conduit could facilitate broadband deployment to areas surrounding such projects.

According to some state, local, and telecommunications officials, planning and flexibility in a dig once policy may help address potential disadvantages by, for example, accommodating states' and localities' existing broadband deployment programs, decreasing the likelihood of installing conduit that will never be used, and giving states the ability to set their own conduit access rates.

For example, officials in one locality said they would like to continue to generate revenue from leasing excess capacity from the city-owned network to private businesses, but they are unsure how a national policy would affect local policy.

Flexibility in a federal policy could also give states the ability to set their own conduit-leasing rates, within reason.

According to some state and industry officials, state DOTs should be able to charge an amount greater than a cost-based rate to fund future conduit expansion and to ensure that costs associated with conduit installation and administration are fully recovered.

AGENCY COMMENTS

We provided a draft of this report to FCC and U.S. DOT for comment. DOT had no comments. FCC provided technical comments, which we incorporated as appropriate.

Susan Fleming Director
Physical Infrastructure Issues

End Notes

[1] The term broadband commonly refers to high speed Internet access. GAO, Telecommunications: Broadband Deployment Is Extensive throughout the United States, but It Is Difficult to Assess the Extent of Deployment Gaps in Rural Areas, GAO-06-426 (Washington, D.C.: May 5, 2006).

[2] H.R. 1695, 112th Cong. (2011); S. 1939, 112th Cong. (2011). As of our reporting date, both bills were pending in Congress.

[3] Throughout this report we refer to "dig once" policies as those broadband deployment policies focused on increasing coordination between government agencies and utility companies to decrease the frequency of highway excavation.

[4] FCC, Connecting America: The National Broadband Plan (Washington, D.C.; Mar. 16, 2010). Also see, GAO, Telecommunications: National Broadband Plan Reflects the Experiences of Leading Countries, but Implementation Will Be Challenging, GAO-10-825 (Washington, D.C.; Sept. 14, 2010) and GAO, Telecommunications: Broadband Deployment Plan Should Include Performance Goals and Measures to Guide Federal Investment, GAO-09-924 (Washington, D.C.; May 12, 2009).

[5] "Long haul transmissions" are transmissions of data over long distances. The infrastructure used for these long haul transmissions includes what are commonly called the Internet "backbone" and "middle mile" fiber, and does not typically provide broadband service to end users.

[6] "Plowing" is a method of installing underground conduit using a plow blade (pulled by a tractor) to provide an opening in the ground. The conduit is then placed at the required depth through a feed tube located on the blade. The dirt is then placed back over the opening to cover the conduit. Plastics Pipe Institute, Second Edition Handbook of PE Pipe, Chapter 14 http://plasticpipe.org/pdf/chapter14.pdf.

[7] "Trenching" is a method of installing underground conduit by which a trench is made using specialized trenching equipment. The conduit is then placed in the ground and the trench is backfilled. Plastics Pipe Institute, Second Edition Handbook of PE Pipe, Chapter 14 http://plasticpipe.org/pdf/chapter14.pdf.

[8] "Boring" (directional boring) is a trenchless method of installing underground conduit using a steerable horizontal drill underneath existing obstacles such as rivers or highways. Plastics Pipe Institute, Second Edition Handbook of PE Pipe, Chapter 14 http://plasticpipe.org/pdf/chapter14.pdf.

[9] Intelligent transportation systems use communications, electronics, sensors, and computer hardware and software to improve the performance or safety of freeway and transit systems that are designed to improve traffic flow. GAO, Intelligent Transportation Systems: Improved DOT Collaboration and Communication Could Enhance the Use of Technology to Manage Congestion, GAO-12-308 (Washington, D.C.: Mar. 19, 2012).

[10] Additional information about this arrangement is provided below.

[11] 23 C.F.R. § 1.23(b),(c).

[12] DOT also noted that, when possible, state and local agencies allow utilities to install facilities, such as conduit, outside of the roadway, which would negate most of the cost savings of installing conduit at the same time as road construction.

[13] 77 Fed. Reg. 36903 (June 20, 2012).

[14] The American Recovery and Reinvestment Act of 2009 established the Broadband Technology Opportunities Program, administered by the Department of Commerce's National Telecommunications and Information Administration to facilitate broadband access to unserved and underserved areas in the United States. Pub. L. No. 111-5, § 6001 (Feb. 17, 2009). Additionally, the Department of Agriculture's Rural Utilities Service established the Broadband Initiatives Program to make loans and award grants for broadband infrastructure projects in rural areas.

[15] U.S. DOT also noted that local agencies currently have the responsibility for determining when, where, and under which conditions utilities are allowed to occupy all public rights-of-way, including those on roadways. As such, these local agencies have the controls and authority to require funding and installation of conduit for broadband services if they determine there is a need.

In: Federal Programs and Policies for Highways   ISBN: 978-1-62257-755-2
Editors: E.D. Campbell and E.Sanchez © 2013 Nova Science Publishers, Inc.

Chapter 7

REVISED FEDERAL STANDARDS
FOR TRAFFIC SIGNS:
FREQUENTLY ASKED QUESTIONS*

David Randall Peterman

SUMMARY

In 2007, the Federal Highway Administration of the Department of
Transportation (DOT) completed a rulemaking to revise the Manual of
Uniform Traffic Control Devices (MUTCD) standard for night-time
visibility (retroreflectivity) of street signs. The new standard set a
minimum measured value for the retroreflectivity of street signs and
required state and local agencies to adopt a method to maintain the
retroreflectivity of their signs. Communities are required to comply with
this standard by 2018.

In 2010, several press reports conflated this new standard with a
2009 MUTCD revised street sign standard—one having to do with the
lettering style of street sign names, which had no compliance deadline—
and became controversial, as the press reports made it appear that the
federal government was requiring communities to replace street signs just
to change their lettering style. This issue has come to the attention of
Congress. In 2011 the DOT proposed to amend the target compliance

---

* This is an edited, reformatted and augmented version of a Congressional Research Service
publication, CRS Report for Congress R41601, from www.crs.gov, prepared for Members
and Committees of Congress, dated September 22, 2011.

date for the retroreflectivity standard (and several other MUTCD standards) to alleviate possible financial burdens the deadlines may create for highway agencies. Agencies will still be required to comply with the retroreflectivity standard. This report answers a number of questions that are frequently asked about this issue.

INTRODUCTION

Since 2007, the Federal Highway Administration (FHWA) of the U.S. Department of Transportation has updated certain national standards for signs on streets and highways.

Recent press reports on this subject have prompted congressional interest. This report addresses some of the questions that have been raised about these standards.

WHAT STANDARDS HAVE BEEN CHANGED?

The FHWA's Manual of Uniform Traffic Control Devices (MUTCD) is a compilation of standards for signs, signals, and design elements of traffic control devices intended to ensure a level of uniformity across the nation.[1]

In 2007, FHWA updated the MUTCD standard governing the maintenance of the night-time visibility (retroreflectivity) of traffic signs (Section 2A.08).

Retroreflectivity refers to the reflection of light back from an object. With respect to traffic signs, this involves reflecting the light from car headlights so that the sign is visible to drivers at night. The 2007 standard set a minimum level of retroreflectivity for signs and required state agencies to adopt methods to ensure that signs met that minimum.

Separately, in the 2009 edition of the MUTCD, FHWA updated the standard concerning the sign lettering style for names of places, streets, and highways (Section 2D.05).

Formerly, names on signs could either be in all capital letters or have only the first letter capitalized. The new standard eliminated the option of using only uppercase letters because studies indicate that mixed-case lettering is easier to read.

WHY WAS THE RETROREFLECTIVITY MAINTENANCE STANDARD CHANGED?

Due to exposure to the elements and other factors, the retroreflectivity of sign materials degrades over time, resulting in signs becoming less visible after dark. In 1992, Congress directed DOT to revise the MUTCD to include "a standard for a minimum level of retroreflectivity that must be maintained for traffic signs and pavement markings which apply to all roads open to public travel."[2] The purpose was to promote public safety by ensuring that traffic signs and pavement markings are visible to drivers after dark.

For many reasons, including the limited visibility of drivers after sunset, driving at night is much more dangerous than driving during the daytime. Nighttime crash rates are estimated to be three times higher than daytime rates, and the fatality rate for nighttime driving is also higher than for daytime driving.[3]

At night, when visual cues available to drivers are much more limited, the assistance provided by street signs becomes more important. For this reason, ensuring that traffic signs are easily seen at night is an important safety consideration. This is of the greatest benefit to older drivers: as people age, the lenses of their eyes typically become less transparent, with the result that more light is needed in order to see objects. The proportion of older drivers is growing as the Baby Boomer cohort ages, making it more important to ensure that signs are easily visible at night.

HOW WAS THE RETROREFLECTIVITY STANDARD SET?

The process of developing the new standard included FHWA-sponsored research and the development of a proposed standard based on that research by a task force appointed by the American Association of State Highway and Transportation Officials (AASHTO), which represents state and local transportation agencies.

FHWA held workshops for members of state and local transportation agencies to publicize the proposed standard, and then revised the proposal through the formal federal rulemaking process from 2004 through 2007, with repeated opportunities for public comment. The new standard took effect on January 22, 2008.

WHAT DOES THE RETROREFLECTIVITY STANDARD REQUIRE?

The new standard involved two elements of maintaining adequate reflectivity. One element was the establishment of numerical standards measuring the minimum acceptable retroreflectivity of signs. Since it was not considered feasible for communities to regularly measure the retroreflectivity of every sign, the second element of the new standard was a requirement that communities adopt a method to maintain the retroreflectivity of their street signs. The standard lists several methods that communities can use to meet this requirement, including

- visual nighttime inspection from a moving vehicle by a trained sign inspector;
- measurement of sign retroreflectivity using a retroreflectometer;
- replacement of signs based on their expected life above the minimum standard for retroreflectivity;
- replacement of all signs in an area, or of a given type, at specified intervals, based on the expected life above the minimum standard for retroreflectivity of the shortest-life material used on the signs in that area or of that type;
- replacement based on the performance of sample signs that are monitored for loss of retroreflectivity; or
- other methods that are developed based on engineering studies.

An agency using a retroreflectivity assessment or management method would be in compliance with the standard even if at times there are individual signs that do not meet the minimum retroreflectivity levels. Finally, this standard requires that communities comply with the new standard by certain deadlines. There are three deadlines:

- January 22, 2012 (four years after adoption of the new standard)—the deadline for communities to have adopted one of the methods to systematically maintain the retroreflectivity of their street signs.
- January 22, 2015 (seven years after adoption)—the deadline for communities to bring all of their regulatory, warning, and post-mounted guide signs (except street name signs and overhead guide signs) into compliance with the new standard.

- January 22, 2018 (10 years after adoption)—the deadline for communities to bring all street name signs and overhead guide signs into compliance.

WAS THE RETROREFLECTIVITY STANDARD CONTROVERSIAL?

Generally, highway safety groups supported the standard, while state and local transportation agencies opposed the establishment of numerical minimum levels of retroreflectivity due to concerns about potential tort liability due to failure to maintain a specific minimum level of retroreflectivity.

They preferred that the standard be limited to establishing a management process that agencies would follow to maintain adequate nighttime visibility of signs.

FHWA's final retroreflectivity standard tried to satisfy both the congressional directive, by including a table of minimum numerical standards in the MUTCD, and the preferences of the state and local transportation agencies, by saying that not every sign needs to meet the minimum standard so long as agencies have a management process in place to maintain the nighttime visibility of their signs.

Regarding tort liability, FHWA noted that having formally implemented a method for maintaining retrroreflectivity would appear to put an agency in a better position to defend lawsuits in which inadequate sign retroreflectivity is an issue.

Also, the final standard provided that agencies that have adopted an assessment or management method will be in compliance even if every individual sign does not meet the minimum retroreflectivity standard.[4]

There appear to be two reasons for the standard's sudden notoriety beginning in the fall of 2010. One is concern on the part of communities about the cost of compliance.

The other, and perhaps more important, reason for the standard's notoriety was that several press reports conflated the retroreflectivity maintenance standard with the entirely unrelated standard concerning lettering, which was modified in the 2009 update of the MUTCD.

WHAT ABOUT THE LETTERING STANDARD?

There is no compliance deadline for the standard on lettering. The lettering standard applies only to signs with names of places, streets, and highways. State and local transportation agencies must implement the new lettering style only as they install new signs or replace existing signs. Some press reports gave the impression that the federal government was requiring communities to immediately begin replacing all street signs just to comply with the new lettering style standard, but this is incorrect.

WHY MUST STATE AND LOCAL AGENCIES COMPLY?

Generally, federal and state laws require that each state adopt a manual of traffic control devices that meets or exceeds the standards in the federal MUTCD. The reason for these requirements is the belief that uniformity in signs and signals promotes public safety.

Most MUTCD standards, such as the lettering standard, do not have compliance deadlines. The case of the retroreflectivity maintenance standard is unusual in this respect. The state and local officials on the AASHTO task force that helped develop the retroreflectivity maintenance standard considered its safety impact to be so significant that they recommended a six-year compliance deadline to ensure that communities implemented the new standard promptly.

WHY MUST PERFECTLY GOOD SIGNS BE REPLACED?

If a traffic sign meets the MUTCD standard for retroreflectivity, it does not have to be replaced. If it does not meet the minimum retroreflectivity standard, then it may create a safety hazard after dark, although it may appear to be perfectly good during daylight hours.

HOW MUCH WILL COMPLIANCE COST?

A study sponsored by the U.S. Department of Transportation estimated the total additional cost to state and local governments to be $37.5 million over a

10-year period. Of this, $27.5 million would be borne by local governments, which are responsible for most traffic signs, and $11.8 million by state governments.[5] The total cost was estimated to represent a 0.5% increase in annual sign maintenance costs for states; data to estimate the incremental impact on local government budgets were not available. The maximum cost in any one year was estimated at $4.5 million. Up to 100% of the cost of replacing traffic signs is eligible for federal funding.

Most larger communities already have sign maintenance and replacement programs; for these communities, the impact of the retroreflectivity maintenance standard is likely to be modest. The impact may be greater in smaller communities that may never have instituted sign maintenance and replacement programs.

Press reports indicate that a number of state and local highway agencies have stated that they estimate their costs to comply with the new standard are much higher than the estimate in the DOT study. The methodologies by which these estimates were generated has not been reported.

IS THE RETROREFLECTIVITY STANDARD AN UNFUNDED MANDATE?

Several comments submitted during the rulemaking process described the rule as an unfunded mandate, as it would impose additional costs on state and local governments for developing sign inventories, training personnel to examine signs, and replacing signs without providing additional resources for this purpose.

Up to 100% of the cost of installing and replacing traffic signs can be covered by federal-aid highway funding. The annual level of federal-aid highway funding provided to states and localities through the annual DOT appropriations act rose from $33.9 billion in FY2004 to $41.1 billion in FY2010, in addition to $27.5 billion provided to states and localities for highway infrastructure investment in the American Recovery and Reinvestment Act of 2009 (P.L. 111-5). Thus, while states did not receive additional federal funding solely for the purpose of implementing the retroreflectivity maintenance standard, the amount of federal highway funding provided to states and localities, from which sign replacement costs could be covered, has increased far more than the estimated increase in cost that the standard would impose.

WHAT IF STATES AND LOCAL GOVERNMENTS DO NOT COMPLY BY THE DEADLINES?

There are two potential enforcement mechanisms for the standards in the MUTCD. First, states and local governments that are not in compliance with the standards are potentially subject to having a portion of their federal transportation funding withheld. However, there is no formal enforcement mechanism to ensure compliance. In fact, one report noted that "It is not uncommon for MUTCD principles to be violated (knowingly or unknowingly) in actual practice."[6]

The more significant potential enforcement mechanism for MUTCD standards is the tort liability that communities may face in the event of a lawsuit involving, in this case, a nighttime car crash in which the visibility of a street sign may be a factor.

CAN THE DEADLINES BE CHANGED OR ELIMINATED?

The deadlines were established through the federal regulatory process, and thus are now regulations. To change or eliminate the deadlines would require either a new rulemaking process or congressional action. DOT has issued a notice of proposed amendments to the compliance deadlines for the retroreflectivity maintenance standard (and numerous other MUTCD standards with compliance deadlines).[7] This could lead to postponement of the compliance deadlines.

DOT proposed to extend the deadline for highway agencies to implement an assessment or management method for ensuring that their signs comply with the retroreflectivity standard, and to limit the scope of that required assessment to regulatory and warning signs, rather than all street signs. DOT also proposed to eliminate the compliance deadlines for replacement of signs that are identified as not meeting the minimum retroreflectivity level standards. Communities are still required to replace any signs that that do not meet the standards.

DOT said it was proposing to change the deadlines to reduce the costs and impacts of the compliance deadlines on state and local highway agencies. It noted that the original deadlines had been based on standard useful-life cycles for signs, but that varying environmental conditions meant that the actual useful life of signs varied in different areas of the country.

Table 1. Proposed Changes to Retroreflectivity Rule

Current Requirements	Proposed Change
Agencies must implement a sign retroreflectivity assessment or management method by January 22, 2012	Deadline extended to two years after effective date of revised Final Rule [approximately January 2014]
Retroreflectivity assessment or management method must be implemented for all traffic signs	Only regulatory and warning signs (e.g., stop signs) must be assessed/managed by the new deadline; other signs must also be assessed, but no deadline.
Noncompliant regulatory, warning, and post-mounted guide signs must be replaced by January 22, 2105	No deadline, though noncompliant signs must be replaced
Noncompliant street name signs and overhead guide signs must be replaced by January 22, 2018	No deadline, though noncompliant signs must be replaced

Source: Federal Highway Administration, National Standards for Traffic Control Devices; MUTCD; Revision, 76 Federal Register 54156, August 31, 2011.

End Notes

[1] States may adopt the national MUTCD as the state MUTCD, adopt the national MUTCD with a state supplement, or adopt a state MUTCD. The supplement or state MUTCD must substantially conform to the national MUTCD; this allows for local exceptions that do not create a safety concern.

[2] P.L. 102-388, Department of Transportation and Related Agencies Appropriations Act, 1993, section 406. FHWA initiated rulemaking on the pavement marking standard in 2010. DOT is implementing the congressional directive in two parts: the traffic sign standard was finalized in 2007, and the rulemaking to implement the pavement marking standard began in 2010.

[3] FHWA, Maintaining Traffic Sign Retroreflectivity: Impacts on State and Local Agencies, April 2007, p. 2.

[4] FHWA, Final Rule, 72 Federal Register no. 245, December 21, 2007, p. 72578.

[5] FHWA, Maintaining Traffic Sign Retroreflectivity: Impacts on State and Local Agencies, FHWA-HRT-07-042, April 2007, p. 25.

[6] FHWA, Minimum Retroreflectivity Levels for Overhead Guide Signs and Street-Name Signs, FHWA-RD-03-082, December 2003, p. 28.

[7] FHWA, 76 Federal Register no. 169, August 31, 2011,54156.

In: Federal Programs and Policies for Highways   ISBN: 978-1-62257-755-2
Editors: E.D. Campbell and E.Sanchez © 2013 Nova Science Publishers, Inc.

Chapter 8

FEDERAL AID TO ROADS AND HIGHWAYS SINCE THE 18TH CENTURY: A LEGISLATIVE HISTORY[*]

John Williamson

SUMMARY

The federal government has provided aid for roads and highways since the establishment of the United States in 1789. This report comprises a brief history of such aid, detailing some precedent setters and more recent funding through the Highway Trust Fund, which was created in 1956.

EARLY ROAD CONSTRUCTION[1]

From the earliest history of the United States, individuals and groups have been lobbying state legislatures and Congress for funds to construct or maintain roads. These Americans believed that roads would encourage both settlement of the country and the movement of goods.

---

[*] This is an edited, reformatted and augmented version of a Congressional Research Service publication, CRS Report for Congress R42140, from www.crs.gov, prepared for Members and Committees of Congress, dated January 6, 2012.

President George Washington was an early advocate of road building in the new United States. As a young man, President Washington had surveyed routes for roads between Virginia and the confluence of the Allegheny, Monongahela, and Ohio Rivers (present-day Pittsburgh, PA), and as a major in the Virginia militia he was tasked with constructing a military road to this strategically important location. On a post-Revolutionary War trip to the West, he met Albert Gallatin, then a young surveyor, who would become a major voice for federal participation in the development of the infrastructure of the United States.

At the end of the 18th century, most roads in the United States were local roads that linked farms to nearby villages, which were often on waterways that were navigable for at least part of the year. Many of these roads were little more than broadened paths that were built and maintained locally, usually by citizens of a community who paid their taxes by working on the roads.

In 1796, Ebenezer Zane successfully petitioned Congress to grant him land (to be surveyed at his own expense) in exchange for building a road and providing ferries to cross the rivers between Wheeling, VA, through the Northwest Territory to the river port of Limestone (now Maysville), Kentucky Territory. Zane's "road" was a wide blazed trail called Zane's Trace, and was later widened and improved by the state of Ohio and became a part of the National Road.

As Secretary of the Treasury in the Jefferson Administration, Albert Gallatin advanced the proposal that states exempt federal land sales from taxation and apply a percentage of the proceeds for road building.[2] Congress adopted this proposal in the Ohio Statehood Enabling Act (2 Stat. 173). The act, signed in 1802, provided that 5% of the proceeds from the sale of public lands in Ohio was to be set aside for roads. In 1803, that act was amended (2 Stat. 225) to provide that 3% of these funds would be available for roads in the state, and 2% would be available for roads to and through Ohio. This form of federal assistance was later extended to all states that had public lands when they were granted statehood.

In March 1807, the Senate directed Secretary Gallatin to prepare a report on the roads and canals existing and proposed in the United States. Gallatin submitted the report to Congress on April 4, 1808. In the summary, Gallatin wrote,

> The early and efficient aid of the Federal [italics in original] Government is recommended by still more important considerations. The inconveniences, complaints, and perhaps dangers, which may result from a vast extent of

territory, can no otherwise be radically removed or prevented than by opening speedy and easy communications through all its parts. Good roads and canals will shorten distances, facilitate commercial and personal intercourse, and unite, by a still more intimate community of interests, the most remote quarters of the United States. No other single operation, within the power of Government, can more effectually tend to strengthen and perpetuate that Union which secures external independence, domestic peace, and internal liberty.[3]

The report recommended an interconnected system of roads, canals, and river improvements be built at federal expense. The plan was opposed in Congress on constitutional, budgetary, and sectional benefit grounds, and was never implemented.[4]

On March 29, 1806, President Thomas Jefferson had signed the Cumberland Road Act (2 Stat. 357). The act directed the President, with the advice and consent of the Senate, to appoint three commissioners to lay out and build a road from the head of navigation on the Potomac River at Cumberland, MD, to a point on the Ohio River. Funding for the project would come from the Ohio 2% fund. The Cumberland Act required that permission be received from the legislatures of Maryland, Virginia, and Pennsylvania before construction could begin. After permission was granted, the road was constructed and named Cumberland Road. It was also known as The National Road.

In 1816, President James Madison proposed federal funding for a system of internal improvements (including roads) in the states, asking that the Constitution be amended to let the federal government finance and construct the projects. A bill to finance internal improvements with funds from a bonus payment from the Bank of the United States passed Congress in 1817. President Madison vetoed the legislation on the last day of his term (March 3, 1817) because the constitution had not been amended.[5]

Over the years after its construction, Cumberland Road deteriorated badly from heavy traffic and a lack of funds for maintenance. Because of the road's deterioration, Congress passed legislation in 1822, which authorized the federal government to collect tolls that would be used for maintenance. President James Monroe vetoed the legislation and stated in his veto message that the collection of tolls implied a power of sovereignty that was not granted to the federal government by the Constitution.[6] Congress provided funding for repairs to the road.

After the election of Andrew Jackson as President in 1828, there was a belief that he would look favorably upon internal improvements. Legislation was introduced to extend the existing Cumberland (National) Road. Jackson vetoed it on the grounds that internal improvements in the states were the affairs of the states. The only other perceived solution was state operation of Cumberland Road as a toll road. In 1831 and 1832, the legislatures of Maryland, Ohio, Pennsylvania, and Virginia agreed to accept and maintain their sections of Cumberland Road.

Jackson believed that as the federal government had complete authority over the territories of the United States, it could construct internal improvements in the territories without restriction. More federal funds were spent on internal improvement projects during the Jackson Administration than in all previous administrations combined—all of it in territories of the United States and the District of Columbia.[7]

BUILDING TOLL ROADS PUBLIC AND PRIVATE

In the absence of significant federal support for highways in the late 18th and early 19th centuries, and with state encouragement and, often, investment, private companies built toll roads in many states. The roads were often financially unsuccessful unless they connected city pairs or provided a farm-or-factory-to-market route with sufficient traffic to cover costs. In discussing the failures of these roads, Secretary Albert Gallatin wrote,

> It is sufficiently evident that, whenever the annual expense of transportation on a certain route, in its natural state, exceeds the interest on the capital employed in improving the communication, and the annual expense of transportation (exclusively of the tolls) by the improved route, the difference is an annual additional income to the nation. Nor does in that case the general result vary, although the tolls may not have been fixed at a rate sufficient to pay to the undertakers the interest on the capital laid out. They, indeed, when that happens, lose; but the community is nevertheless benefited by the undertaking.8

The boom in turnpike construction began in the late 1790s and lasted, with a roughly 10-year interruption in the 1830s, until the mid-19th century.[9] By 1830, more than 8,000 miles of roads had been built or converted to turnpikes under state charters of incorporation. Very few toll roads made consistent profits for their investors and the failure rate appears to have been high even in the early years predating rail and canal competition. Despite these financial difficulties, the toll roads were, without a doubt, the best roads in the country, and had a significant role in short- and medium-distance freight and passenger movement between the cities and larger towns. With the spread of the railway networks, however, the toll roads lost nearly all their passenger and most of their freight business to rail competition. As the longer turnpikes failed, shorter toll roads were chartered as feeder lines to rail service.

By 1900, most turnpike companies had gone out of business. State and local governments took over some of these roads in an orderly fashion and assumed the responsibility for maintenance of these routes. On a good number of roads, however, turnpike companies, in the face of financial failure, simply ceased operations and abandoned their roads. Because of the perceived chaos caused by what was seen as capricious abandonment of turnpikes, toll roads were often held in low regard. State turnpike legislation in the late 19th century generally included provisions for the dissolution of toll companies and the orderly transfer of responsibility to state or local governments.[10]

The resistance to federal financial involvement in "internal improvements," such as roads, was based, in part, on constitutional concerns, discussed earlier, and also on budgetary constraints and state/regional rivalries.[11] The budget of the United States was dependent on tariff revenues and was quite small by modern standards, and some feared a major commitment to road construction could overwhelm the budget.[12] Sectional differences and state and regional rivalries also played a major role in the resistance to federal spending on roads because of concerns that federal road construction would benefit other states or regions more.

THE GOOD ROADS MOVEMENT

With the invention of the modern bicycle and pneumatic tires in the late 1880s, bicycles rapidly became very popular. The less than ideal road conditions of the time, however, made bicycling laborious and even dangerous. The growth of cyclist organizations led to the establishment in 1892 of the National League for Good Roads, whose purpose was to coordinate the Good Roads Movement and lobby governments at all levels to improve the condition of roads. It was reported that farmers, feeling that they should not be taxed so city dwellers could enjoy a bicycle ride in the country, were not at first a part of this movement. After road lobbyists began working with the Post Office while it was developing Rural Free Delivery, farmers began participating in the push for road improvements. The Good Roads

Movement had a profound influence on the states' initiation of state aid for the creation of highway departments and commissions.[13]

On March 3, 1893, Benjamin Harrison, in one of his last acts as President, signed the 1894 Department of Agriculture Appropriations Act (27 Stat. 737). This act gave the Secretary of Agriculture $10,000 to research road construction and management. The appropriation was made to the Secretary of Agriculture because it was believed that many farmers were not able to transport their produce to railroad terminals or nearby towns in a timely fashion because of inadequate or otherwise poor quality roads. The Secretary created the Office of Road Inquiry (ORI) to conduct the research.

For several years after its inception, the duty of the ORI was to collect information and disseminate it through lectures, publications, and consultations, but a new program was added in 1896: short stretches of road would be built using contributed and borrowed labor and other resources. The only federal costs of this project were the salary and expenses of an ORI road expert who would design and supervise the work. The ORI was renamed the Office of Public Road Inquiries (OPRI) in 1899. Appropriations for roads increased in 1901 and continued to increase almost every year; by 1912 appropriations were over $160,000. In 1905, Congress created the Office of Public Roads (OPR) to "furnish expert advice on road building; to make investigations in regard to the best methods of road making, and the best kinds of road-making materials in the several states; to investigate the chemical and physical character of road materials."[14] Congress had become concerned about the constitutionality of federal funds going to roads wholly within individual states, but groups such as the National League for Good Roads, the American Roads Builders, the American Highway Association, and the National Highway Association were determined to secure legislation to increase federal aid to roads. In conjunction with their efforts, more than 60 bills were introduced calling for federal aid to roads during the first six months of the second session of the 62nd Congress (December 1911-May 1912).

The Post Office Department Appropriations Act 1913 (P.L. 62-336, 37 Stat. 539) appropriated $500,000 to be expended by the Secretary of Agriculture, in conjunction with the Postmaster General, to aid in the improvement of rural-area post roads. The act stated that the funds would be available to state or local governments that agreed to pay two-thirds of the construction costs, but did not specify how the funds were to be distributed among the states. Ultimately, 13 states and 28 counties participated, and approximately 455 miles of road were built. Experience under this legislation led to OPR's decision that federal aid should go solely to the states, and not to the counties. The act also provided for the establishment of the Joint Committee on Federal Aid in the Construction of Post Roads to consider the problem of road maintenance. On November 25, 1914, the committee released a report entitled *Federal Aid to Good Roads*.[15] The report did not make specific recommendations, but did support the proposition that Congress should grant more federal funds to road construction.[16] The committee defended the constitutionality of its recommendation by saying that it would aid in establishing post roads, regulating commerce, providing for common defense, and promoting general welfare.[17]

State highway officials joined together in 1914 to form the American Association of State Highway Officials (AASHO) to provide assistance to the federal government on legislative, technical, and economic subjects relating to highways.

Following the beginning of World War I in July 1914, European powers began purchasing large quantities of supplies from the United States. As more and more goods were moved to ports in the United States and Canada for shipment, the nation's railroad system became overloaded. This increased demand for the rapid movement of goods and the existence of a network of roads led to the rapid development of the trucking industry. On April 6, 1916, the United States entered World War I and the amount of goods moving by truck expanded exponentially.

During 1914 and 1915, the nation's roads deteriorated rapidly under the increased use by heavy trucks. In response, AASHO members drafted a bill and submitted it to Congress. The bill was only four pages in length and called for increased federal financial assistance for highways. The Federal-Aid Highway Act of 1916 was signed into law by President Woodrow Wilson on July 11, 1916, as P.L. 64-156 (39 Stat 355). The act

- appropriated funds for the construction of rural post roads;
- stated that state participation in the program was permissible, but that any state that chose to participate must comply with the legislation's provisions;
- made it clear that the authority and responsibility of initiating projects was reserved to the states, and that federal participation was dependent upon approval by federal authority;
- stipulated that the state highway department or its equivalent would represent the state in its administration of the program;

- appropriated $10 million for the construction of roads and trails within national forests for FY1917-FY1926 at a rate of $1 million per year; and
- provided the basic policy for the development of main roads serving federally owned lands, reservations, or areas.

In 1918, the Office of Public Roads was renamed the Bureau of Public Roads (BPR) and specifically charged with administering federal funding of road construction.

The Federal-Aid Highway Act of 1921 (P.L. 67-87, 42 Stat. 212) divided highways into two categories: primary (interstate) and secondary (intercounty). It also gave limited federal aid to a system of highways to be designated by each state, not to exceed 7% of the state's total mileage. The act stated that each state would be responsible for maintaining the highways constructed with federal funds, and that failure to do so would result in the work being done under direct federal supervision with funds which would otherwise be available to that state for construction.

Congress saw highway and road building as a job stimulant when the economy soured in 1929 and responded by increasing funds for construction of more highways and roads. In April 1930, Congress voted to amend the Federal Aid Highway Act of 1916 and authorized and appropriated $50 million in addition to the $75 million already authorized and appropriated for FY1931. The act also provided $125 million for road construction in FY1932 and FY1933 (P.L. 71-90, 46 Stat. 141).

The Federal-Aid Highway Act of 1938 (P.L. 75-584, 52 Stat. 633) called for a study of the feasibility of a national network of superhighway toll roads. The resulting study, *Toll Roads and Free Roads*,[18] concluded that "the construction of direct toll highways cannot be relied upon as a sound solution of the problem of providing adequate facilities for ... necessary highway transportation of the United States or to solve any considerable part of this problem."[19]

THE 1940S TO THE PRESENT: A LEGISLATIVE HISTORY OF FEDERAL AID TO ROADS

The Roosevelt Administration was planning for the post-war period before official American involvement in World War II began. On April 14, 1941,

President Franklin D. Roosevelt appointed the National Interregional Highway Committee to study the possibility of creating a unique system of highways with all necessary connections through and around cities that would meet the immediate requirements of the War Department and the future needs of increased postwar traffic. This system was to be administered by the newly named Public Roads Administration (formerly the BPR). The committee sent its report to Congress in January 1944.[20]

The Federal-Aid Highway Act of 1944 (P.L. 78-521, 58 Stat. 838) provided for the designation of a National System of Interstate Highways by federal and state officials, not to exceed 40,000 miles, unless additional mileage was necessary. No funds, however, were authorized or appropriated for the interstate highway system. Instead, the act appropriated $225 million for primary roads in each of the first three post-war years, $150 million for secondary and feeder road projects, and $125 million for urban federal-aid highway construction. The act established apportionment formulas for each state.

Although an Interstate Highway System had been proposed in 1913 by the National Highway Association,[21] the Federal-Aid Highway Act of 1952 (P.L. 82-413, 66 Stat. 158), which authorized $25 million for the Interstate system on a 50% federal-50% state matching basis, was the first law to allot funds specifically for Interstate construction. President Dwight D. Eisenhower was instrumental in implementing the Interstate Highway System, adding a specific national defense dimension to the concept, among other things.

The Federal-Aid Highway Act of 1954 (P.L. 83-350, 68 Stat. 70) authorized $175 million for the interstate system for FY1956, and $175 million for FY1957, both to be used in a 60-40 federal-state matching ratio.

In 1956, federal aid for highways increased dramatically with the passage of the Federal Aid Highway and Highway Revenue Acts of 1956 (P.L. 84-627, 70 Stat 374). The act authorized an additional $1 billion for FY1957, $1.7 billion for FY1958, and $2 billion for FY1959. The act created the Highway Trust Fund to ensure a source of financing for the National System of Interstate and Defense Highways. Since that time, tax revenues have been directed to the Highway Trust Fund derived from excise taxes on highway motor fuel and truck-related taxes on the sale of truck tires, trailers, and heavy vehicles. (For an overview of the trust fund activities, see *Table 1.*) Prior to the creation of the trust fund, federal financial assistance to highways came from the general fund of the U.S. Treasury. Although federal motor fuel and motor vehicle taxes existed prior to the creation of the trust fund, the receipts were directed to the general fund, and no formal relationship existed between federal funding for highways and these taxes. The 1956 act originally set the expiration date for the crediting of these funds to highway funding at the end of FY1972; however, subsequent legislation has extended the imposition of the taxes and their transfer to the trust fund until September 30, 2012.[22]

The Federal-Aid Highway Act of 1959 (P.L. 86-342, 73 Stat 611) extended the National System of Interstate and Defense Highways to Alaska and Hawaii and stated the intent of Congress to reimburse every state for portions of highways absorbed into the Interstate System that were built after August 2, 1947, and contracted for completion by June 30, 1957.

The Federal-Aid Highway Act of 1962 (P.L. 87-866, 76 Stat. 1145) created the continuing, comprehensive, cooperative (3C) transportation planning process, which required states and local communities to develop long-range highway plans and programs in urban areas of more than 50,000 population and to properly coordinate the programs with the programs for other forms of transportation.

The Highway Safety Act of 1966 (P.L. 89-564, 80 Stat. 731) required that each state have a highway safety program, authorized by the Secretary of Transportation, designed to reduce deaths, injuries, and property damage. In 1966, Congress passed the Department of Transportation Act (P.L. 89-670, 80 Stat. 931), which changed the name of the BPR to the Federal Highway Administration (FHWA) and moved the FHWA into the newly created Department of Transportation.

The federal share of non-interstate highway projects was increased from 50% to 70% under the Federal-Aid Highway Act of 1970 (P.L. 91-605, 84 Stat. 1713), which also created the Special Bridge Replacement Program (SBRP). The act directed the Secretary to inventory bridges on the national highway system, "classify them according to their serviceability, safety, and essentiality for public use; and based on that classification, assign each a priority for replacement." The act further stated that states' requests for funding for bridge replacement would be funded from the priorities in the SBRP inventory. The federal share of bridge replacement would be up to 75%.

The Federal-Aid Highway Act of 1973 (P.L. 93-87, 87 Stat. 250) authorized funds to complete the Interstate Highway System, which it named the National System of Interstate and Defense Highways. This act also apportioned funds for the construction of bus lanes and highway traffic control devices, set a national policy for priority for other roads in the federal-aid highway system, and included a provision that allowed states to use a limited amount of highway funds for the construction of separate bicycle lanes, bicycle facilities, and pedestrian walkways. The act also permitted states to request funding for fixed-rail transit facilities in lieu of highway construction, with the amount to be equal to the amount that would have been furnished for the highway construction, but with funds to be drawn from the general fund rather than the Highway Trust Fund.

The 1976 Federal-Aid Highway Act (P.L. 94-280, 90 Stat. 425) established the "resurfacing, restoration, and rehabilitation" (3R) program which, for the first time, allowed federal funds to be used for resurfacing, restoration, and rehabilitation of existing highways. The Surface Transportation Assistance Act of 1978 (1978 STAA) (P.L. 95-599, 92 Stat. 2689) expanded and transformed the Special Bridge Replacement Program into the Highway Bridge Replacement Program to include repair as well as replacement, and it authorized appropriations for theresurfacing of interstate highways that had been in use for more than five years. The eligibility requirements for the 3R program were revised in the Federal-Aid Highway Act of 1981 (P.L. 97- 134, 95 Stat. 1701). This act also prohibited a state from receiving less than one-half of 1% of the total apportionment for the Interstate System.

The availability of advance construction funds to bridge projects under the highway bridge replacement and rehabilitation program was extended under the Surface Transportation Assistance Act of 1982 (1982 STAA) (P.L. 97-424, 96 Stat. 2097). This act also permitted states to transfer funds allocated for a particular urbanized area to another such area. Under this act, the apportionment of highway funds was reduced for states that did not require proof of payment of heavy vehicle use tax before such vehicle could be registered in the state. The act also established a Disadvantaged Business Enterprises (DBEs) program to guarantee 10% of monies spent on projects to businesses certified as being economically or socially disadvantaged. Several important features of this act dealt with the highway trust fund, including a tax increase (gasoline tax up 5 cents per gallon to 9 cents per gallon) and the mass transit account, which was established within the Highway Trust Fund (effective April 1, 1983).

The 1982 STAA also required that emergency relief funds be appropriated from the Highway Trust Fund and authorized appropriations for FY1983 through FY1986 out of the Highway Trust Fund for bridge replacement and rehabilitation and projects aimed at eliminating hazards.

The Surface Transportation and Uniform Relocation Assistance Act of 1987 (STURAA) (P.L. 100-17, 101 Stat. 132) authorized appropriations out of the Highway Trust Fund for FY1988 through FY1993 for highway assistance projects. STURAA was the only highway bill to be vetoed by a President in the 20th century, being vetoed by President Ronald Reagan.[23] The act was passed over his veto (by 350-73 in the House, and by 67-33 in the Senate). The act increased the limit on emergency relief grants for each state from $30 million to $100 million and permitted them to use a certain percentage of their Interstate Highway transfer funds for highway planning and research.

On December 18, 1991, the Intermodal Surface Transportation and Equity Act of 1991 (ISTEA) (P.L. 102-240, 105 Stat. 2038) was signed into law. The act declared that the authorizations of appropriations and apportionments for the Interstate Highway System made by it were to be the last authorizations of appropriations and apportionments for the completion of the system. ISTEA also established the Surface Transportation Program (STP) to fund projects such as construction, reconstruction, rehabilitation, resurfacing, restoration, and operational improvements for highways and bridges, bike transportation, pedestrian walkways, and transportation enhancement activities anywhere on the federal-aid system. The STP program allowed spending on roads that many in the transportation community previously considered to be below the federal level of responsibility. These changes were magnified by a broadening of the states' abilities to transfer other highway program funds to STP.

HIGHWAYS UNDER TEA-21

On June 9, 1998, the Transportation Equity Act for the 21st Century (TEA-21) (P.L. 105-178, 112 Stat. 107) was signed into law. In addition to reauthorizing revenue streams for the Highway Trust Fund until FY2005, TEA-21 also authorized highway program funding at a level of approximately $218 billion for FY1998 through FY2003. A minimum guarantee was enacted to guarantee each state at least 90.5% of its contributions to the highway trust fund.[24] TEA-21 also amended the Balanced Budget and Emergency Deficit Control Act of 1985 (P.L. 99-177, 99 Stat. 1037) by creating two new categories within the discretionary budget: highway and transit. These so-called firewalls for highway and transit funds prevented appropriators from reducing these programs to increase spending on other programs. Of the $218 billion authorized by TEA-21, 81% ($177 billion) was for highways and highway safety programs. Most of the remaining 19% ($41 billion) was to be used for transit. Under TEA-21, each state was guaranteed at least 90.5% share returns on the funds the state's highway users paid into the trust fund. TEA-21 eliminated the payment of interest on the unexpended balance of the highway trust fund. In the past, these interest payments were very controversial, being viewed as simply a transfer of funds, because the interest was coming from the general fund of the U.S. Treasury. Not only did TEA-21 eliminate interest payments, but it also called for the transfer of the unexpended balance of the Highway Trust Fund to the general fund over the amount of $8 billion as of September 30, 1998.

One extremely important mechanism of TEA-21 was the Revenue Aligned Budget Authority (RABA).[25]

RABA ensures that highway spending is directly proportional to highway revenues, so if highway revenues are projected to increase, so does highway spending and vice versa. RABA provided an additional $9 billion for highway spending between FY2000 and FY2002, and then in FY2003, after the RABA adjustment, the amount available for highway spending dropped 30%. In response, Congress included language in the Consolidated Appropriations Act, 2003 (P.L. 108-7, 117 Stat. 11), which raised highway spending for FY2003 to $31.8 billion.

HIGHWAYS UNDER SAFETEA-LU

The Safe, Accountable, Flexible, Efficient, Transportation Equity Act: A Legacy for Users (SAFETEA-LU) (P.L. 109-59, 119 Stat. 1144) became law on August 10, 2005.

The act modified and extended the funding guarantees created in TEA-21 through the life of the legislation (FY2005 through FY2009). Under SAFETEA, the RABA adjustment was altered to be based on the average of actual receipts from two years prior and receipt projections for the current year, allowing a negative adjustment only when the Highway Trust Fund is below $6 billion. RABA funds were only distributed in FY2007 ($842 million).

SAFETEA-LU also broadened somewhat the ability of states to use tolling on interstate highways for traffic congestion reduction and to finance construction. In addition, the legislation cleared up questions that had arisen about the use and operation of high-occupancy vehicle (HOV) lanes on federally funded highways.

The Equity Bonus (EB) Program replaced the Minimum Guarantee (MG) Program found in TEA-21.

The EB Program guarantees that states receive an annual percentage floor relative to the TEA-21 average annual apportionment.

Several pilot programs were also authorized in the legislation:

- the *Truck Parking Facilities Program* is intended to deal with the paucity of long-term parking for commercial vehicles along the National Highway System;
- *Highways for Life Program* provides funding to improve safety, decrease construction time, reduce congestion from construction, and improve the driving experience;
- the *Real-Time System Management Information Program* is intended to provide states the capability to monitor major highways in real time and use the information to mitigate or reduce congestion; and
- the *Future Strategic Highway Research Program* is to be run by the National Research Council of the National Academy of Sciences to research renewal of highway infrastructure with minimum delay of traffic, prevent or reduce the severity of highway crashes, reduce travel times, and integrate other concerns into enlarging highway capacity. The program received $205 million for FY2006 through FY2009.

Since October 1, 2009, federal aid to highways has been operating on a series of authorization extension acts.

Table 1. Status of the Highway Account of the Trust Fund
(thousands of dollars)

Fiscal Year	Expenditures	Closing Balance	Fiscal Year	Expenditures	Closing Balance
1957	$965,667	$516,335	1984	10,384,239	10,210,493
1958	1,511,603	1,048,534	1985	12,756,149	10,360,790
1959	2,612,576	523,657	1986	14,180,359	9,485,989
1960	2,940,251	119,221	1987	12,801,838	9,411,559
1961	2,619,170	299,063	1988	14,037,862	9,019,108
1962	2,783,864	470,661	1989	13,602,480	10,550,999
1963	3,016,701	746,926	1990	14,375,194	9,628,954
1964	3,645,013	641,431	1991	14,686,495	10,245,943
1965	4,026,117	284,858	1992	15,517,751	11,300,224
1966	3,965,431	243,535	1993	16,640,749	11,523,292
1967	3,973,426	725,196	1994	19,010,855	9,517,301
1968	4,171,110	981,572	1995	19,472,496	9,421,424

Fiscal Year	Expenditures	Closing Balance	Fiscal Year	Expenditures	Closing Balance
1969	4,150,575	1,520,827	1996	19,995,345	12,117,818
1970	4,378,253	2,611,611	1997	20,856,750	12,575,718
1971	4,685,348	3,651,696	1998	20,347,235	16,535,084
1972	4,690,217	4,489,531	1999	23,134,686	19,206,256
1973	4,811,036	5,590,688	2000	26,999,828	22,553,544
1974	4,599,013	7,666,652	2001	29,098,372	20,371,688
1975	4,843,089	9,597,390	2002	32,218,581	16,136,043
1976	6,520,603	9,076,650	2003	32,109,031	12,991,384
1977	6,147,175	10,163,646	2004	31,968,892	10,807,494
1978	6,057,737	11,672,503	2005	33,121,424	10,592,258
1979	7,154,141	12,564,460	2006	33,912,089	9,014,017
1980	9,212,311	10,999,460	2007	34,979,234	8,110,431
1981	9,173,762	9,259,443	2008	37,011,932	10,032,229
1982	8,035,206	9,046,417	2009	37,571,317	8,881,338
1983	8,837,637	9,061,618	2010	32,006,716	20,743,269

Source: Federal Highway Administration, Highway Statistics 2010.

End Notes

[1] A broad overview of highway and road construction, and a source of some material in this report, is U.S. Department of Transportation, Federal Highway Administration, America's Highways, 1776-1976: A History of the Federal-Aid Program (Washington: GPO, 1977), 560 p.

[2] Albert Gallatin, Letter to Hon. Mr. Giles, Chairman of the Committee on the admission of the Northwestern Territory into the Union, Washington, Feb. 13,1802, in Walter Lowrie and Matthew St. Clair Clarke, eds. American State Papers, Volume I, 7th Cong., 1st sess. (Washington: Gales & Seaton, 1833), pp. 327-328.

[3] American State Papers, vol. I, 10th Cong., 1st sess., p. 725.

[4] Pamela L. Baker, "The Washington National Road Bill and the Struggle to Adopt a Federal System of Internal Improvement," Journal of the Early Republic, vol. 22, no. 3 (Autumn 2002,) p. 440; George Rogers Taylor, The Transportation Revolution, 1815-1860 (Armonk, NY: M.E. Sharpe, Inc., 1977), pp. 17-22.

[5] Annals of Congress, 14th Cong., 2nd sess., 1059-1061.

[6] U.S. House of Representatives, Message from the President of the United States With His Objections to the Bll for the Preservation and Repair of the Cumberland Road; Also, a Paper containing his Views on the subject of Internal Improvements (Washington: Gales & Seaton, 1822), 60 p.

[7] Pamela L. Baker, The National Road and the Promise of Improvement, 1802-1850 (Chicago: Univ. of Illinois at Chicago, Ph.D. dissertation, 2003), p. 49.

[8] American State Papers, Volume I, p. 724.

[9] Joseph A. Durrenberger, Turnpikes; A Study of the Toll Road Movement in the Middle Atlantic States and Maryland (Cos Cob, CT.: J.E. Edwards, 1968), 188 p.

[10] Durrenberger, Turnpikes; A Study of the Toll Road Movement in the Middle Atlantic States and Maryland, 188 p.

[11] John Larson, Internal Improvement: National Public Works and the Promise of Popular Government in the Early United States, 1783-1863 (Chapel Hill: University of North Carolina Press, 2001), 324 p.; Taylor, The Transportation Revolution, 1815-1860, pp. 15-22. See also: America's Highways: 1776-1976: A History of the Federal-Aid Program, pp. 16-27.

[12] U.S. Department of Commerce, Bureau of the Census, Historical Statistics of the United States: Colonial Times to 1970 (Washington: GPO, 1975), p. 1106. Total federal revenues were $10.8 million in 1800, $24.8 million in 1830, and $56 million in 1860.

[13] U.S. DOT, FHWA, America's Highways, 1776-1976: A History of the Federal-Aid Program, p. 41; Philip P. Mason, The League of American Wheelmen and the Good Roads Movement, 1880-1905 (University of Michigan: Ph.D. dissertation, 1957), 274 p.

[14] U.S. Congress, Committees on Appropriations of the Senate and House of Representatives, Appropriations Made During the First Session of the Fifty-Ninth Congress (Washington: GPO, 1906), p. 30.

[15] U.S. Congress, Joint Committee on Federal Aid in the Construction of Post Roads, Federal Aid to Good Roads (Washington: GPO, 1914), 204 p.

[16] Ibid., p. 13.

[17] Ibid., pp. 14-16.

[18] U.S. Congress, House, Toll Roads and Free Roads. On the Feasibility of a System of Transcontinental Toll Roads and a Master Plan for Free Highway Development, April 27, 1939, H.Doc. 272 (Washington: GPO, 1939), 170 p.

[19] Ibid., p. 4.

[20] U.S. Congress, House, Interregional Highways, H.Doc. 379 (Washington: GPO, 1944), 214 p.

[21] Richard F. Weingroff, "Good Roads Everywhere: Charles Henry Davis and the National Highways Association," found at U.S. Department of Transportation, Federal Highway Administration, Highway History, last modified April 7, 2011, http://www.fhwa.dot.gov/infrastructure/davis.cfm.

[22] For an overview of the history of the Interstate Highway System, see Earl Swift, The Big Road (New York: Houghton Mifflin Harcourt, 2011).

[23] U.S. Congress, House. Veto of H.R. 2, Message from the President (Washington: GPO, 1987), 135 p.

[24] CRS Report R41869, The Donor-Donee State Issue in Highway Finance, by Robert S. Kirk.

[25] For a further discussion of the effects of RABA, see CRS Report RS21164, Highway Finance: RABA's Double-edged Sword, by John W. Fischer.

INDEX